ONE-HOUR CHRISTMAS CRAFTS

*T*his holiday season, craft your way to a merry Christmas with quick and easy handmade treasures. Inside One-Hour Christmas Crafts, you'll find more than 90 projects that will impress people on your gift list and visitors to your delightfully decorated home. All our creations can be made in less than 60 minutes — some in less than 10! Oh, what fun you'll have fashioning snuggly wearables and spirited accents for friends, family, and home. And by using this guide, which is part of our Clever Crafter series, you'll have plenty of time to enjoy the pleasures of this captivating season. Simply turn the pages to get your holidays off to a crafty start!

Anne Childs

LEISURE ARTS, INC.
Little Rock, Arkansas

ONE-HOUR CHRISTMAS CRAFTS

EDITORIAL STAFF

Vice President and Editor-in-Chief: Anne Van Wagner Childs
Executive Director: Sandra Graham Case
Design Director: Patricia Wallenfang Sowers
Editorial Director: Susan Frantz Wiles
Publications Director: Kristine Anderson Mertes
Creative Art Director: Gloria Bearden
Senior Graphics Art Director: Melinda Stout

DESIGN
Designers: Katherine Prince Horton, Sandra Spotts Ritchie, Anne Pulliam Stocks, Linda Diehl Tiano, and Rebecca Sunwall Werle
Executive Assistants: Debra Smith and Billie Steward
Design Assistant: Melanie Vaughan

TECHNICAL
Managing Editor: Sherry Solida Ford
Senior Technical Writer: Laura Lee Powell
Technical Writer: Christopher M. McCarty
Technical Associates: Jennifer L. Hobbs and Susan McManus Johnson
Production Assistant: Sharon Heckel Gillam

EDITORIAL
Managing Editor: Linda L. Trimble
Coordinating Editors: Terri Leming Davidson and Janice Teipen Wojcik
Associate Editor: Stacey Robertson Marshall

ART
Book/Magazine Graphics Art Director: Diane M. Hugo
Senior Production Graphics Artist: Michael A. Spigner
Photography Stylists: Pam Choate, Sondra Daniel, Laura Reed, Beth Carter, Aurora Huston, and Courtney Jones

PROMOTIONS
Managing Editors: Alan Caudle and Marjorie Ann Lacy
Associate Editors: Steven M. Cooper, Dixie L. Morris, Jennifer Ertl Wobser, and Ellen J. Clifton
Designer: Dale Rowett
Art Director: Linda Lovette Smart
Production Artist: Leslie Loring Krebs
Publishing Systems Administrator: Cynthia M. Lumpkin
Publishing Systems Assistants: Susan Mary Gray and Robert Walker

BUSINESS STAFF

Publisher: Rick Barton
Vice President and General Manager: Thomas L. Carlisle
Vice President, Finance: Tom Siebenmorgen
Retail Sales Director: Richard Tignor
Vice President, Retail Marketing: Pam Stebbins
Retail Marketing Director: Margaret Sweetin
General Merchandise Manager: Cathy Laird

Vice President, Operations: Brian U. Davis
Distribution Director: Rob Thieme
Retail Customer Service Director: Tonie B. Maulding
Retail Customer Service Managers: Carolyn Pruss and Wanda Price
Print Production Manager: Fred F. Pruss

Library of Congress Catalog Number 98-65189
International Standard Book Number 0-8487-6118-9

Table of Contents

Table of Contents

ONE-HOUR DECORATING 40

Table of Contents

ONE-HOUR TREE TRIMMING 72

ONE-HOUR GIFTS

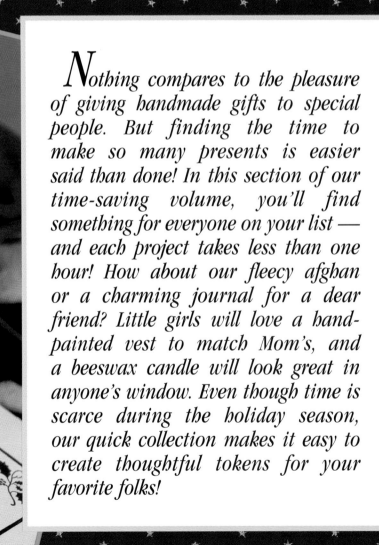

*N*othing compares to the pleasure of giving handmade gifts to special people. But finding the time to make so many presents is easier said than done! In this section of our time-saving volume, you'll find something for everyone on your list — and each project takes less than one hour! How about our fleecy afghan or a charming journal for a dear friend? Little girls will love a hand-painted vest to match Mom's, and a beeswax candle will look great in anyone's window. Even though time is scarce during the holiday season, our quick collection makes it easy to create thoughtful tokens for your favorite folks!

IN ONLY **15** *MINUTES!*

*A*dd a classy touch to a muslin-covered frame with pearl trim and painted stars. It takes just minutes to glue on the beaded trim! For the gold stars, use a paint pen to draw the designs on the frame.

PEARL FRAME

You will need: 5" x 7" muslin-covered picture frame, flatback pearl trim, gold paint pen, and a hot glue gun and glue sticks.

1. Measure width and length of frame; cut two lengths of pearl trim for each of the determined measurements.

2. Glue pearl trim to frame; allow to dry.

3. Use paint pen to draw stars on frame.

DAZZLING DECOUPAGED PLATES

DECOUPAGED PLATES

What an impressive gift!
Friends and family will love serving
their cookies in customized style.
In no time, you can prepare these
dazzling plates by decoupaging clear
glass dishes with pretty paper napkins
or Christmas cards.

For each plate, you will need: clear glass plate, Christmas card, foam paintbrush, sponge piece, and decoupage glue.

For cardinal plate, you will also need: Christmas paper napkin.

For tree plate, you will also need: cream and metallic gold acrylic paint.

(**Note:** Use plates for dry foods only; wipe clean with damp cloth.)

1. Cut design from Christmas card front and trim as desired. Follow glue manufacturer's instructions to decoupage card to back of plate.

2. For cardinal plate, use foam brush to apply a thin coat of decoupage glue to entire back of plate. Place napkin wrong side up over glue; smooth in place, working out air bubbles. Allow to dry to the touch. Trim edge of napkin even with edge of plate. Apply a second coat of glue over napkin.

3. For tree plate, refer to *Painting Basics* (pg. 104) and use sponge to lightly apply cream, then metallic gold paint to back of plate, allowing to dry between colors.

TRIMMED YULETIDE TOWELS

Dainty ruffles, offset with gold cord, highlight these bright red, fluffy bath towels. In less than half an hour, you can stitch a merry trim for one of these handsome towels. This lovely gift would also look wonderful in your own bathroom!

RUFFLED TOWELS

For each towel, you will need: red bath towel, pinking shears, $1/3$ yd. of Christmas fabric, gold cord, and metallic gold thread.

1. Measure width of towel; multiply by $1\frac{1}{2}$. Use pinking shears to cut fabric $5\frac{1}{2}$"w by the determined measurement. Cut one length of cord the same width as towel.

2. Matching right sides and long edges, fold fabric strip in half. Stitch along each short end of strip; turn right side out and press.

3. Baste $1/4$" from pinked edge of fabric strip. Pull thread to gather fabric to fit width of towel; knot thread ends and trim. Pin ruffle to towel; baste in place. Use metallic thread and a zigzag stitch to sew gold cord over basting.

10

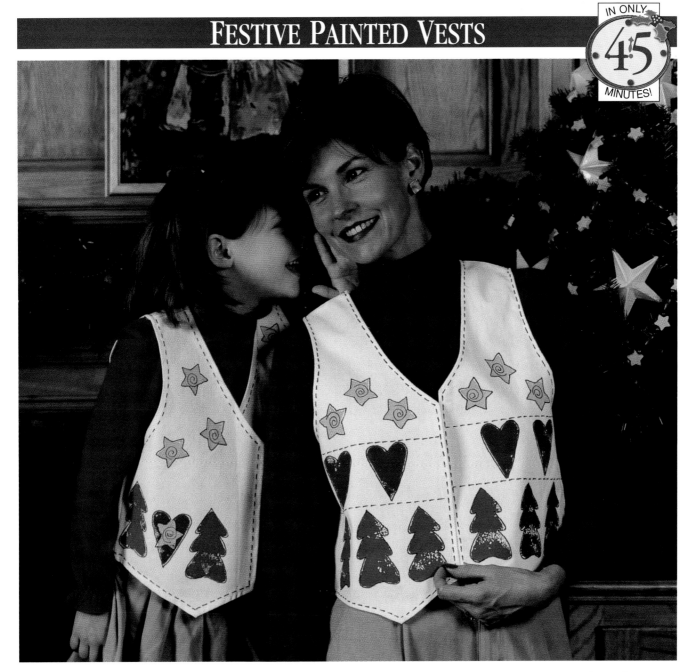

*F*estive fashions for the exciting days of Christmas, these cute canvas vests make great casual wear for adults and kids! Colorful designs are stamped onto purchased garments using shaped sponges for a quick-and-easy finish.

CANVAS VESTS

You will need: tracing paper; compressed craft sponge; one adult-size and one child-size canvas vest; yellow, red, and green acrylic paint; and a black fabric marker.

1. Trace vest star, vest tree, and vest heart patterns (pg. 107) onto tracing paper; cut out. Use patterns to cut shapes from compressed sponge.

2. Referring to *Painting Basics* (pg. 104), use sponge shapes to stamp designs on vest fronts; allow to dry.

3. Use marker to draw "stitches" and designs on stars, and to outline trees, stars, and hearts.

11

*D*isplaying cherished photos on bright memory album pages is a fun, creative way to remember those special holiday moments. Acid-free papers guarantee that precious snapshots will be protected from discoloring, and merry background papers add pizzazz.

MEMORY PAGES
You will need: tracing paper; transfer paper; stylus; yellow, parchment, and red acid-free paper; tree and star-shaped craft punches; hole punch; photos; acid-free Christmas papers; gold paint pen; acid-free album pages; colored pencils; pinking shears; black pen; and a glue stick.

1. Trace ornament A (pg. 122) and pull-toy horse (pg. 110) patterns onto tracing paper; cut out.

2. For ornament page, use pattern to cut one shape each from parchment and red paper.

3. Use punches to cut shapes from desired paper. Trim photo to fit center of ornament. Arrange cutouts and photo on Christmas paper; glue in place. Use gold paint pen to draw designs and ornament hanger on red ornament. Glue Christmas paper to album page.

4. For pull-toy horse page, use stylus to transfer pattern to parchment paper; cut out slightly outside drawn line. Use pencils to color design.

5. Use star punch to cut shapes from yellow paper.

6. For photo backgrounds, use pinking shears to cut red paper $3/8$" larger all around than photos. Center photos on backgrounds and glue in place. Use pen to draw designs around borders.

7. Arrange photos, stars, and horse on Christmas paper and glue in place. Use black pen to draw pull string on horse. Glue Christmas paper to album page.

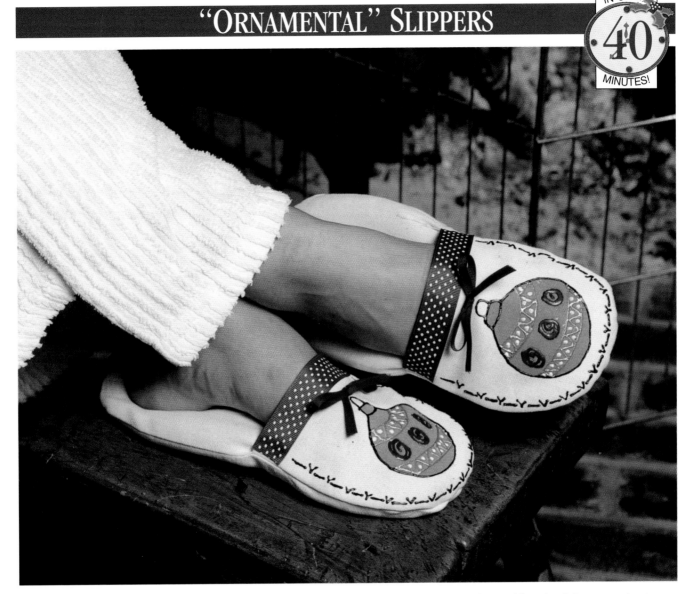

*H*elp a friend slip into comfort with our jolly hand-painted house shoes. The colorful Christmas ornament motifs are trimmed with dimensional paint. Ribbon accents make the pair as cute as they are cozy!

YULETIDE SLIPPERS

You will need: tracing paper; canvas slippers; paintbrush; green acrylic paint; white, gold metallic, red, and black dimensional paint; 1/2 yd. of 1/4"w red grosgrain ribbon; 1/3 yd. of 1"w green and white polka-dot grosgrain ribbon; and a hot glue gun and glue sticks.

1. Trace slipper ornament pattern (pg. 107) onto tracing paper; cut out.

2. Draw around pattern on each slipper. Paint ornaments green; allow to dry. Use white, gold, and red dimensional paint to decorate ornaments as desired. Use black dimensional paint to outline ornaments, to draw hangers, and to draw designs around sides and toes of slippers.

3. Cut red ribbon in half; tie each length into a bow. Glue one bow above hanger of ornament on each slipper.

4. Cut two 5" lengths of green ribbon; glue one length to edge of each slipper top.

13

Elves aren't the only helpers Santa will have this Christmas! Dress up a youngster North-Pole style with a vibrant holiday smock. Easily fashioned by adding a felt collar and iron-on letters to a ready-made smock, this fun top will protect kids' clothes during the making and baking of the Yuletide season.

SANTA'S HELPER SMOCK

You will need: tracing paper, $^1/_3$ yd. of green felt, child-size smock, red thread, red baby rickrack, $^3/_4$" red felt iron-on letters, red embroidery floss, and $^1/_2$" dia. jingle bells.

1. Remove loop side of hook and loop fastener from smock; set aside.

2. Referring to *Making Patterns* (pg. 104), trace collar pattern (pg. 108) onto tracing paper. Use pattern to cut collar from felt. Sew collar to neckline of smock.

3. Cut a length of rickrack to fit around neckline. Sew rickrack in place over collar. Replace loop fastener over collar.

4. Cut an apostrophe shape from one spare letter. Arrange letters and apostrophe to spell SANTA'S HELPER on front of smock; follow manufacturer's instructions to fuse in place.

5. Use six strands of red embroidery floss to sew one jingle bell to each point of collar. Knot floss and trim ends, leaving $^1/_2$" tails.

IN ONLY 35 MINUTES!

*F*riends and family will love keeping snapshots of all their shining stars in this easy-to-make scrapbook. Our special album is decorated with only a few scraps of felt, embroidery floss, buttons, and glue. It's sure to be a treasured keepsake for years to come.

STAR-BRIGHT SCRAPBOOK
You will need: 12¼" x 14¼" red scrapbook; pinking shears; 12" x 14" piece of gold felt; tracing paper; 9¾" x 12" piece of black felt, green felt piece; scraps of brown and gold felt; gold, red, and brown embroidery floss; embroidery needle; four brown buttons; and fabric glue.

1. Use pinking shears to cut an 11" x 13¼" rectangle from gold felt.

2. Referring to *Making Patterns* (pg. 104), trace tree, tree trunk, and star patterns (pg. 109) onto tracing paper. Use patterns to cut one tree from green felt, one star from gold felt, and one tree trunk from brown felt.

3. Arrange tree, tree trunk, and star on black felt piece; glue edges of shapes in place. Allow to dry.

4. Referring to *Embroidery Stitches* (pg. 105), use three strands of gold floss to work Straight Stitches for stars on tree, and three strands of red floss to work French Knots on star and tree. Use three strands of brown floss to work Running Stitch around edge of tree trunk.

5. Center black rectangle over gold rectangle and glue in place. Center gold rectangle on scrapbook and glue in place.

6. Glue a button to each corner of black rectangle.

15

This whimsical snowman sweatshirt is a perfect warmer for chilly days — and it's oh-so-easy to make! Using clear nylon thread to stitch around the fused-on appliqués eliminates the need to change thread colors with each fabric. A pinned-on scarf gives a jaunty finish.

FROSTY SWEATSHIRT

You will need: paper-backed fusible web, scraps of white and black fabric and orange felt, sweatshirt, clear nylon thread, black embroidery floss, 1" dia. red button, two ³/₄" dia. black buttons, white dimensional paint, 3" x 12" torn fabric strip for bow, and a safety pin.

1. Referring to *Fusing Basics* (pg. 104), use patterns (pg. 113) to make snowman head, nose, and hat appliqués. Arrange appliqués on sweatshirt front and fuse in place.

2. Use nylon thread and a narrow zigzag stitch to sew around edges of appliqués.

3. Referring to *Embroidery Stitches* (pg. 105), use black floss and work Straight Stitches for mouth on snowman. Sew red button on hat and black buttons on face for eyes.

4. Referring to *Painting Basics* (pg. 104), use dimensional paint to paint dots and snowflakes on sweatshirt front; allow to dry.

5. For scarf, tie knot at center of torn fabric strip. Use safety pin on wrong side of sweatshirt front to attach scarf.

CHRISTMAS CANDLE LIGHT

*F*olks *on your gift list can add a touch of nostalgia to their homes with this charming beeswax candle lamp. Since the lamp is quick and easy to assemble (just 15 minutes for one lamp), plan on preparing a bunch for friends and relatives!*

BEESWAX CANDLE LAMP

You will need: battery-powered candle lamp, honeycomb beeswax sheet, 24" length of 1³/₈"w ribbon, 2" length of floral wire, two 16" lengths of jute twine, and a small sprig of artificial greenery.

1. Measure height and circumference of candle; add 1" to circumference. Cut a piece of beeswax sheet the determined measurement. Wrap beeswax around candle, overlapping edges and pressing to seal.

2. Fold ribbon to form a double-loop bow; secure at center with wire. Trim ends of ribbon.

3. Using both lengths of jute twine, tie ribbon bow to base of candle; tie ends of jute into bow.

4. Insert end of greenery sprig into knot in jute.

17

STARRY STEMWARE

*E*legant yet easy to make, our festive wine glass provides a glamorous way to toast the holiday season! You can create this frosty effect in just 20 minutes — simply apply etching cream over star and dot stickers, then rinse! It's fun to fashion stemware for family members or create distinctive glassware for a favorite couple.

FINE WINE GLASS
You will need: a ¹/₈" hole punch, self-adhesive star stickers, wine glass, and etching cream.

1. Use hole punch to cut dots from self-adhesive sticker material between star stickers.

2. Apply star and dot stickers to glass.

3. Follow manufacturer's instructions to apply etching cream. Rinse glass; remove stickers.

IN ONLY 22 MINUTES!

*A*dd an air of enchantment to an extra-special present by tucking it in our elegant gift bag! Embellished with a lacy doily, gold berries, and charms, the outside of this lovely container will make friends and relatives eager to discover what's inside! It takes just over 20 minutes to turn a white gift bag into an eye-catching wrapper personalized with an embroidered monogram.

ELEGANT GIFT BAG

You will need: wrapping paper, white gift bag, gold paint pen, small crocheted or tatted doily, angel and heart-shaped charms, assorted buttons, assorted lace and braid trims, monogram letter, $1^1/_2$ yds. of $1^1/_2$"w white wired ribbon, gold berry sprigs, and a hot glue gun and glue sticks.

1. Cut a rectangle of wrapping paper $^1/_2$" smaller on all sides than front of gift bag. Center on front of bag; glue in place.

2. Use paint pen to draw a border $^1/_4$" outside edges of wrapping paper.

3. For flap, fold top 2" of bag to front.

4. Cut doily in half. Press $^1/_2$" of cut edge to wrong side of doily. Align folded edge of doily with folded edge at top of flap; glue doily in place.

5. Arrange trims, buttons, letter, and charms on front of gift bag; glue in place.

6. Referring to *Multi-Loop Bows* (pg. 106), tie ribbon into a multi-loop bow. Insert berries through knot in bow. Glue bow over doily near fold at top of flap.

7. Lift flap to place gift in bag.

JOLLY SNOWMEN GIFT BAGS

IN ONLY 28 MINUTES!

*B*undle your hard-to-wrap presents in our pretty yet practical gift carriers! It's amazingly easy to add jolly sponge-painted snowmen and perky grosgrain ribbon trim to sturdy brown shopping bags. In less than 30 minutes, your clever gift totes are ready to hold exciting surprises for special friends!

CHEERY GIFT BAGS

You will need: tracing paper; compressed craft sponge; white acrylic paint; paper plate; two 8" x 10" brown paper gift bags; white, red, orange, and brown dimensional paint; 16" length of red polka-dot grosgrain ribbon; and glue.

Note: Refer to *Painting Basics* (pg. 104) for all painting.

1. Trace large snowman pattern (pg. 112) onto tracing paper; cut out. Use pattern to cut shape from compressed sponge.

2. Use sponge and white acrylic paint to paint snowmen on bags; allow to dry.

3. Use dimensional paints to paint scarf, nose, buttons, face, and arms on each snowman. Use white dimensional paint to paint snow on bags.

4. Cut ribbon length in half; glue one half to top front edge of each bag.

EASIEST-EVER COASTERS

*O*rdinary cork coasters become handy holiday helpers when they're decorated with holly motifs created with easy-to-use paint pens. They're inexpensive and super-quick to make, so you can craft sets for all your friends!

FESTIVE COASTERS

You will need: tracing paper; transfer paper; stylus; coasters with cork liners; white, red, and green paint pens; and clear acrylic spray sealer.

1. Trace holly with berries pattern (pg. 108) onto tracing paper. Use transfer paper and stylus to transfer design to each coaster.

2. Allowing to dry between coats, use paint pens to color designs.

3. Spray designs with one coat of sealer; allow to dry.

21

ADORABLE BABY BIB

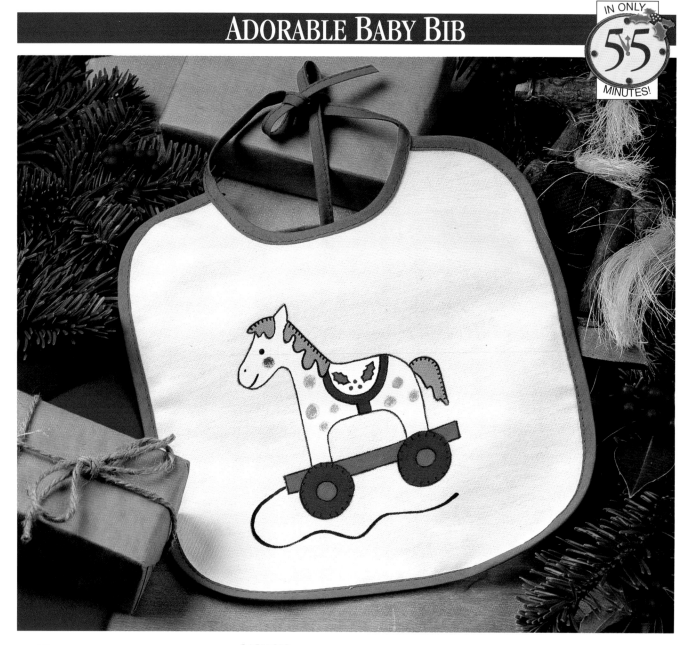

*O*ur *bib will show Santa what's on baby's wish list! This infant necessity will look adorable while it keeps the little one's holiday finery looking its best. All you do is transfer the pattern to a ready-made bib and paint away!*

BABY BIB
You will need: tracing paper; iron-on transfer pen; white fabric bib; white, ivory, red, green, tan, and black acrylic paint; paintbrushes; black permanent pen; and a pencil with an unused eraser.

1. Using tracing paper and transfer pen, follow pen manufacturer's instructions to transfer pull-toy horse pattern (pg. 110) to center of bib.

2. Use color key (pg. 110) to paint design on bib.

3. Use black pen to outline design and add details.

4. Use pencil eraser to paint dots and cheek on horse.

22

*M*ake any snack merrier by serving a warming beverage in one of these crafty cups. To quickly create the clever designs, use colored pencils to tint rubber-stamped images. Contrasting paper behind the punched stars or pinked edge provides a festive background.

FESTIVE MUGS

For each mug, you will need: rubber stamp; black ink pad; one piece of white cardstock and one piece of red or green cardstock, each measuring $3^1/2$" x $10^1/2$"; colored pencils; star punch or pinking shears; clear plastic coffee mug with insert; and a glue stick.

1. To make decorative mug liner, stamp white cardstock as desired; allow ink to dry. Use pencils to color designs.

2. Punch stars or use pinking shears to trim $1/2$" from bottom of white cardstock. Matching edges, glue decorated cardstock to red or green cardstock; allow to dry.

3. Remove insert from mug. Place liner inside mug and replace insert.

SNOW FLURRY PILLOWCASES

*S*noozing on our eye-catching pillowcases will inspire visions of light, lacy snowflakes dancing against the wintry sky. The dark green cases are edged with stenciled snowflakes and jumbo rickrack.

SNOWFLAKE PILLOWCASES
For each pillowcase, you will need: stencil plastic, craft knife, stencil brush, white fabric paint, dark green pillowcase, white jumbo rickrack, and white sewing thread.

1. Trace large and small snowflake patterns (pg. 108) onto stencil plastic. Use craft knife to cut out stencil segments along drawn lines.

2. Referring to *Painting Basics* (pg. 104), use stencil and fabric paint to paint snowflakes along hem of pillowcase; allow to dry.

3. Measure across end of pillowcase; add 1". Cut a length of rickrack the determined measurement. Turning ends of rickrack under ¹/₂", sew rickrack to pillowcase along hem seam.

COZY SNOWMEN SWEATSHIRT

*S*prinkle a festive frosting of holiday fun across the front of this dashing sweatshirt! To achieve the charming effect, sponge paint the snowmen, add accents using dimensional paints, and spatter paint the falling snow.

SNOWMEN SWEATSHIRT

You will need: tracing paper, compressed craft sponge, paper plate, white fabric paint, sweatshirt, toothbrush, paper towel, and assorted colors of dimensional paint.

Note: Refer to *Painting Basics* (pg. 104) for all painting.

1. Trace large snowman pattern (pg. 112) onto tracing paper; cut out. Use pattern to cut shape from sponge.

2. Use sponge shape to paint snowmen on front of sweatshirt; allow to dry.

3. Use dimensional paint to add faces, scarves, buttons, arms, and snow details to sweatshirt; allow to dry.

4. To spatter paint on sweatshirt, dip toothbrush bristles into fabric paint. Blot bristles on paper towel to remove excess paint. Holding toothbrush just above sweatshirt, pull thumb across bristles; allow paint to dry.

IN ONLY
41
MINUTES!

*S*anta's little helper will be as pretty as a Christmas tree when she wears this festive jumper! It's simple to "trim" a child's dress with rickrack "garland," fused-fabric ornaments, and perky plaid bows.

CHRISTMAS CUTIE'S DRESS
You will need: child's green fleece jumper, yellow baby rickrack, paper-backed fusible web, scraps of yellow and red fabrics, gold and red dimensional paint, $1^1/_3$ yds. of $1^1/_2$"w plaid ribbon, fabric glue, and three small safety pins.

1. Arrange rickrack on front of dress; glue in place.

2. Referring to *Fusing Basics* (pg. 104), use ball ornament and ornament top patterns (pg. 107) to make four appliqués each from red and yellow fabrics. Arrange appliqués on dress front and fuse in place.

3. Referring to *Painting Basics* (pg. 104), use gold dimensional paint to outline each ornament top and to draw hanger. Use red dimensional paint to outline each ornament.

4. Cut ribbon into three 15" lengths. Tie each length into a bow. Use safety pin on wrong side of dress to attach each bow to front of dress.

VERSATILE HOLIDAY BASKET

*O*ur versatile holiday basket has both decorative and practical appeal. Filled with pinecones, it's perfect as part of a Yuletide centerpiece. The fabric-wrapped basket can also be an extra-special holder for greeting cards or a charming way to deliver seasonal treats!

JINGLE BELL BASKET
You will need: woven basket, string, pencil, thumbtack, Christmas fabric, polyester fiberfill, large rubber band, pinking shears, 5/8"w grosgrain ribbon, large jingle bell, and a hot glue gun and glue sticks.

1. Measure basket from rim to rim as shown in Fig. 1; multiply by 1¹/₂ to determine diameter of fabric circle. Cut a square of fabric 2" larger than the determined diameter.

Fig. 1

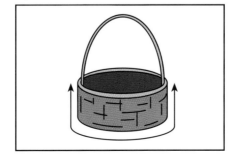

2. Use fabric square and follow *Cutting a Fabric Circle* (pg. 106) to cut a circle with the diameter determined in Step 1.

3. Center basket on wrong side of fabric circle. Bring edges of fabric up and secure around rim of basket with rubber band, adjusting gathers evenly. Tuck fiberfill into fabric around sides of basket for desired fullness.

4. Use pinking shears to trim fabric 1" above rim of basket.

5. Wrap ribbon around basket, covering rubber band; knot ribbon and trim ends.

6. Glue jingle bell to knot of ribbon.

27

IN ONLY
10
MINUTES!

*M*ake the season merrier for folks on your list by crafting colorful containers to hold tasty gifts. Holiday stickers and paint pens let you have a ball decorating these buckets in record time — just 10 minutes each — including the wired-ribbon bows on top!

TREAT BUCKETS

For each bucket, you will need:
Christmas stickers, plastic bucket with handle and lid, red and green paint pens, 1¹/₂ yds. of 1"w wired gingham ribbon, a hot glue gun and glue sticks, and desired treats.

1. Place stickers on bucket as desired. Use paint pens to add message, swirls, dots, and stars; allow to dry.

2. Cut a 20" length of ribbon; tie into a bow. Glue bow to handle; trim ends.

3. Fill bucket with treats.

28

MERRY MINI TOTES

IN ONLY 35 MINUTES!

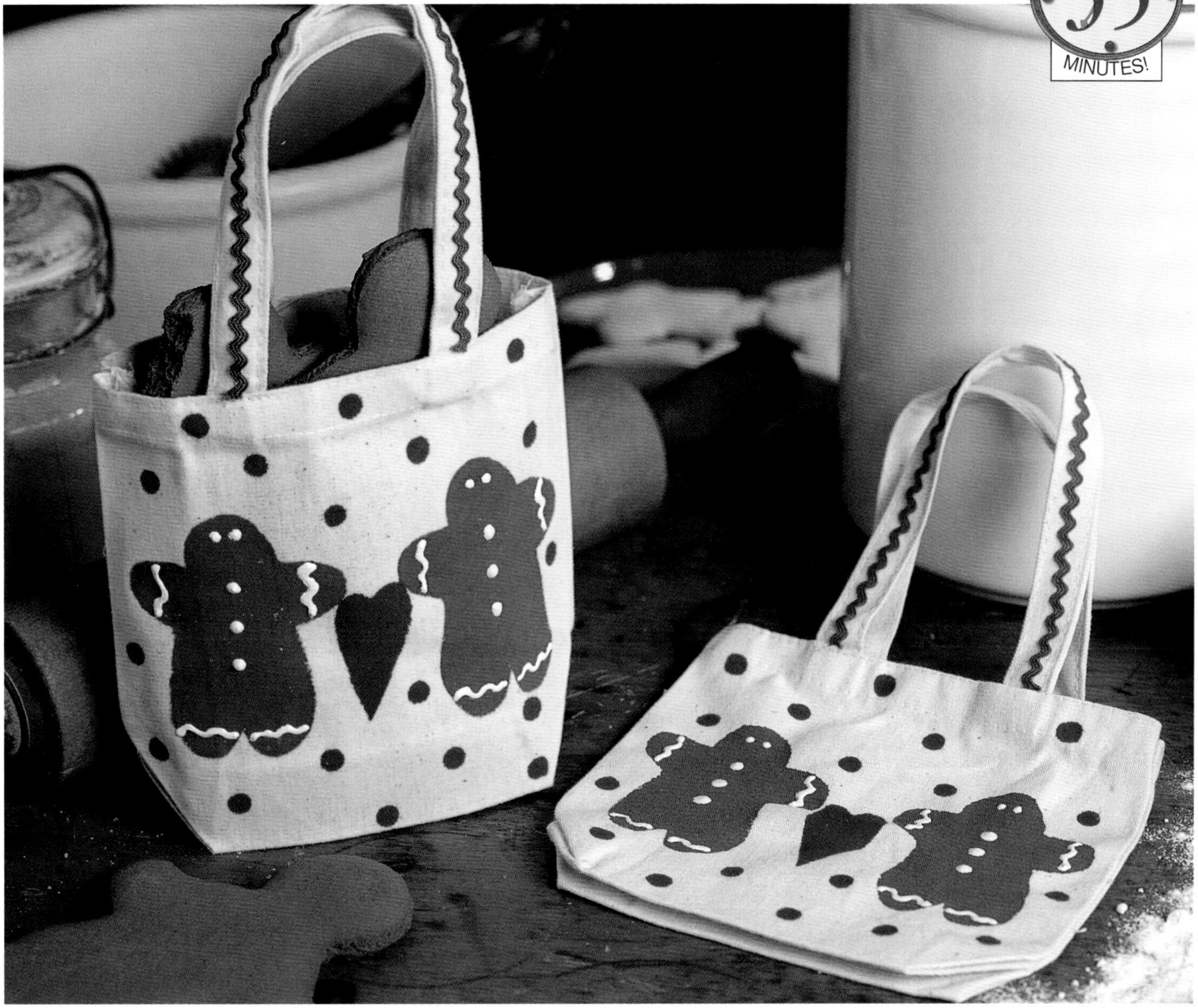

Mini totes are terrific gifts for friends and neighbors — especially when they're filled with special treats! Using easy painting techniques and rickrack trim, you can decorate ready-made bags in no time.

GINGERBREAD MAN MINI TOTE

For each tote, you will need: green baby rickrack, green sewing thread, canvas mini tote bag, tracing paper, sharpened pencil with unused eraser, brown and red acrylic paint, paintbrushes, and white dimensional paint.

1. Cut two pieces of rickrack the same length as tote handle; sew one length along center of each handle.

2. Trace gingerbread man and heart patterns (pg. 111) onto tracing paper; cut out. Use pencil to draw around patterns on front of tote.

3. Paint gingerbread men brown and heart red. Use pencil eraser dipped in red paint to stamp dots on tote. Allow paint to dry.

4. Referring to *Painting Basics* (pg. 104), use dimensional paint to add details to gingerbread men; allow to dry.

GINGERBREAD FOOTSTOOL

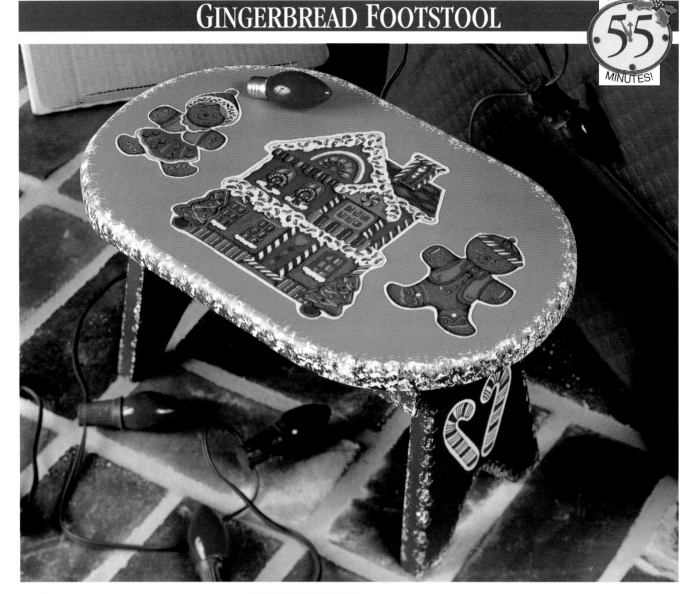

*W*ith a multitude of uses, this charming gingerbread footstool is as handy as it is decorative! Simple painting techniques and fabric appliqués make this project a darling addition to any Yuletide home.

HOLIDAY FOOTSTOOL

You will need: fine grit sandpaper; tack cloth; unfinished wooden footstool; sponge paintbrush; white, green, and tan matte-finish paint; sponge piece; paper-backed fusible web; ¼ yd. of fabric with Christmas motifs; and acrylic spray sealer.

1. Use sandpaper to lightly sand surface of stool; use tack cloth to remove dust.

2. Applying two coats and allowing to dry between coats, paint top of stool tan. Paint base and legs of stool green.

3. Referring to *Painting Basics* (pg. 104), use a sponge piece to lightly stamp edge of stool top with green paint; allow to dry. Lightly stamp all edges of stool with white paint.

4. Refer to *Fusing Basics* (pg. 104) to make appliqués using Christmas motifs from fabric.

5. Arrange appliqués on top and legs of stool; fuse in place.

6. Spray stool with sealer.

This embellished box will keep goodies safe for Santa! The background fabric and cookie motifs are fused to the top of a papier-mâché box, and the "icing" details are added with dimensional paint. The jolly elf will find a sweet surprise when he peeks inside!

SANTA'S COOKIE BOX

You will need: 6" square papier-mâché box, paper-backed fusible web, scraps of assorted fabrics, parchment paper, hole punch, red embroidery floss, pinking shears, 3/4"w fusible web tape, black felt-tip pen, white and brown dimensional paint, and glue.

1. Referring to *Fusing Basics* (pg. 104), use gingerbread man, tag, heart, and cookie patterns (pg. 111) to make appliqués from desired fabric scraps.

2. For paper tag, cut 3" x 4" pieces of parchment paper and fusible web. Fuse web to wrong side of paper; do not remove paper backing. Center and fuse tag appliqué to right side of fused paper. Trim paper 1/4" outside appliqué. Fuse heart appliqué to tag. Punch a hole in point of tag; thread a 4" length of floss through hole and tie to secure.

3. Fuse web to a 6" square of fabric. Use pinking shears to trim 1/4" from edges of square.

4. Arrange tag, cookie, and gingerbread man appliqués on fabric square; fuse in place. Center and fuse square to top of box lid.

5. Use pen to write "Cookies for Santa" on tag and to draw designs on box.

6. Referring to *Painting Basics* (pg. 104), use dimensional paint to decorate cookies.

7. Fuse web tape to a 1" x 26" strip of coordinating fabric. Pink long edges of strip; fuse to sides of box lid, overlapping ends.

8. Tie a 1" x 12" strip of coordinating fabric into a bow; glue to front side of lid.

IN ONLY
30
MINUTES!

*H*ere's a nifty gift that's also a decorative place to stash things during the holidays. This papier-mâché box is a stellar hideaway for holiday snapshots, Christmas knickknacks, or candy. Fused-on fabric and basic painted designs make the project a snap to do.

STAR BOX

You will need: 12¹/₂"w star-shaped papier-mâché box, newspaper, red spray paint, 4"w wooden star, paintbrush, one 13" square each of paper-backed fusible web and Christmas print fabric, green acrylic paint, black medium-point marker, six ³/₄" dia. green buttons, and a hot glue gun and glue sticks.

1. Remove lid from box.

2. Place bottom of box upside down on newspaper. Use red spray paint to paint box bottom and wooden star; allow to dry.

3. Referring to *Fusing Basics* (pg. 104), fuse web to wrong side of fabric; do not remove paper backing. Place box lid on paper side of fused fabric; draw around lid. Cut out shape ¹/₄" inside drawn line. Center appliqué and fuse to box lid.

4. Use green paint to add stripes to sides of lid; allow to dry. Use marker to draw designs on sides of lid.

5. Center wooden star on lid; glue in place. Glue one button to each point of lid and one button to top of wooden star.

DANDY APPLE CANDLE

*O*ur homemade candle will warm a friend's heart with the country charm of apples. It's created by filling a "recycled" jar with melted wax and topping it with a ring of dried apple slices. A torn-fabric bow provides the finishing touch.

DANDY APPLE CANDLE

You will need: newspaper, candle wax or wax crystals, large can, saucepan, wire cutters, heavy gauge craft wire, small glass jar, wax-coated candle wick, dried apple slices, 1" x 26" torn fabric strip, button, and a hot glue gun and glue sticks.

1. (**Caution**: Do not melt wax in saucepan placed directly on burner.) Cover work area with newspaper. Place wax in can. Place can in saucepan; fill saucepan half full with water. Heat water until wax melts.

2. Measure around mouth of jar; add 1". Use wire cutters to cut two lengths of craft wire the determined measurement. Wrap one wire around rim of jar, twisting ends to secure. For jar handle, cut an 8" length of wire. Thread handle ends through rim wire; twist to secure.

3. Measure height of jar; add 1". Cut a length of wick the determined measurement. Fill jar with melted wax to within 1" of top; allow to harden slightly. Insert wick into wax, centering in jar.

4. Cut apple slices into small pieces; thread pieces onto remaining cut length of wire. Wrap wire around rim of jar; twist ends to secure.

5. Tie fabric strip into a bow around jar; glue button over knot of bow.

This no-fuss gift will inspire a holly-jolly holiday! Using silk holly leaves makes quick work of the appliquéd letters. Just follow our easy method for fusing the leaves in place, then add a bow and acrylic-jewel "berries."

HOLLY JOY SWEATSHIRT

You will need: silk holly with small leaves, aluminum foil, paper-backed fusible web, ecru sweatshirt, red acrylic jewels, 1"w red satin ribbon, safety pin, and jewel glue.

1. Remove holly leaves from stem.

2. Referring to *Fusing Basics* (pg. 104), follow Foil Method to fuse web to holly leaves.

3. Arrange holly leaves on sweatshirt front to spell out JOY; fuse in place.

4. For berries, follow glue manufacturer's instructions to glue jewels to leaves; allow to dry.

5. Tie ribbon into a bow; use safety pin on wrong side of shirt front to attach bow.

IN ONLY 40 MINUTES!

As cute as a button, our spirited snowman necklace and festive pins are easy to fashion! Make each in only 40 minutes or less. This colorful jewelry is also easy on your pocketbook when made using felt scraps and treasures from your button box.

BUTTON JEWELRY

You will need: scraps of white, gold, blue, red, and green felt; assorted buttons; tracing paper; and craft glue.

For snowman necklace, you will also need: red, brown, and black embroidery floss; black and yellow fine-point markers; and three large white buttons (ours measure $^3/_4$" dia., 1" dia., and $1^1/_8$" dia.) for snowman.

For wreath pin, you will also need: red and green embroidery floss, pinking shears, and a pin back.

For tree pin, you will also need: white embroidery floss and a pin back.

Snowman Necklace

1. Arrange large buttons for snowman on blue felt. Use red embroidery floss to sew buttons for body in place. Referring to *Embroidery Stitches* (pg. 105), use black floss to sew on button for head by working French Knots for eyes. Position buttons for hands on felt and use brown floss to stitch in place. Use long stitches between hands and body for arms.

2. Trace hat, hat trim, and pom-pom patterns (pg. 126) onto tracing paper; cut out. Use patterns to cut pieces from gold and red felt. Arrange hat pieces on blue felt and glue in place; allow to dry. Use markers to draw mouth and nose.

3. Trim blue felt $^1/_8$" outside edges of snowman.

4. Cut three pieces of embroidery floss the desired length for necklace; place pieces together. Knotting floss between stacks of buttons, thread buttons onto floss. Glue center of necklace to back of snowman head; allow to dry.

5. Place snowman and necklace on white felt piece and glue in place; allow to dry. Trim white felt $^1/_8$" outside edges of blue felt, using care not to cut floss.

Wreath Pin

1. Trace wreath A and wreath B patterns (pg. 126) onto tracing paper; cut out. Use patterns and pinking shears to cut wreaths from felt.

2. Use embroidery floss to sew buttons to wreath A. Use two colors of embroidery floss to make bow for top of wreath A. Glue bow to wreath; allow to dry.

3. Center and glue wreath A to wreath B; allow to dry.

4. Glue pin back to back of wreath; allow to dry.

Tree Pin

1. Trace tree A, tree B, tree C, and tree trunk patterns (pg. 126) onto tracing paper; cut out. Use patterns to cut tree pieces from felt. Arrange pieces on white felt and glue in place; allow to dry. Work Running Stitch (pg. 105) along edges of tree and trunk.

2. Use embroidery floss to sew buttons to tree as desired. Trim white felt $^1/_8$" outside edges of tree. Glue tree to red felt; allow to dry. Trim red felt $^1/_8$" outside edges of white felt.

3. Glue pin back to back of tree; allow to dry.

Chase away the chills with this cuddly winter warmer! To whip up the cozy wrap, just add felt holly leaves, perky red buttons, and quick running stitch embroidery to a thermal fleece afghan.

HOLLY LEAF AFGHAN

You will need: tracing paper, green felt piece, thermal fleece afghan with blanket-stitched edges, black embroidery floss, and five ³/₄" dia. red buttons.

1. Trace holly leaf pattern (pg. 114) onto tracing paper; cut out. Use pattern to cut seven leaves from felt.

2. Arrange leaves around one corner of afghan; pin in place. Referring to

Embroidery Stitches (pg. 105), use embroidery floss and work Running Stitch to sew leaves to afghan.

3. For berries, use embroidery floss to sew buttons between leaves.

4. Trace "S" pattern (pg. 114) twice onto tracing paper. Pin patterns to afghan. Use embroidery floss to work Running Stitch through paper; carefully tear away tracing paper.

These festive frames will certainly provide a jolly outlook for the holidays! Simply glue novelty miniatures to a pair of eyeglasses and add a string of colorful beads.

HOLIDAY SPECS

You will need: eyeglasses with green frames, assorted miniature wooden Christmas shapes, wooden bead garland, wide rubber band, needle, clear nylon thread, and glue.

1. Glue Christmas shapes to frames of eyeglasses.

2. Leaving enough string to tie a knot at ends, cut a 30" length of bead garland.

3. Cut two 1" lengths from rubber band. Fold each length in half and use needle and thread to sew through ends to form a loop. Sew one rubber band loop to each end of garland.

4. Slip rubber band loops over temples of eyeglasses.

Spruce up a tasteful and ever-popular gift by tucking a bottle of wine in an easy-to-make wrapper. You can make two bags from one kitchen towel, then complete the cordial look with bells, bows, and wintry flourishes.

WINE BAGS

You will need: one large kitchen towel, thread to match, two 20" lengths of $2^{1}/_{8}$"w wired ribbon, floral wire, two 35mm jingle bells, and two sprigs of artificial greenery.

1. With right sides together, fold towel in half lengthwise. Using a $^{1}/_{2}$" seam allowance, sew long edges of towel together. Matching short edges, fold towel in half; mark towel along fold. Unfold towel and stitch $^{1}/_{2}$" from each side of mark. Cut towel in half along mark.

2. Turn bags right side out. Place a bottle in each bag.

3. Gathering top of each bag around bottle neck, tie in place with wired-ribbon bow. Thread floral wire through knot to secure bell to bow; tuck greenery sprig behind ribbon.

IN ONLY
20
MINUTES!

A very special friend will love having a crafty place to record holiday memories. In just minutes, you can create a rustic volume with a wintry touch by gluing frayed fabric shapes and buttons onto a blank journal.

SNOWMAN JOURNAL
You will need: 5" x 7" blank book or journal, tracing paper, scraps of white and orange fabric for snowman, 4³/₄" x 6¹/₄" and 3¹/₂" x 5" torn fabric rectangles, black pen, ¹/₂" x 7" torn fabric strip for scarf, four ³/₈" dia. green buttons, and craft glue.

1. Trace circle A, circle B, circle C, and nose patterns (pg. 111) onto tracing paper; cut out. Use patterns to cut pieces for snowman from fabric; fray edges of circles.

2. Center large rectangle on front of journal and glue in place. Center small rectangle on large rectangle and glue in place. Arrange pieces for snowman on small rectangle and glue in place. Use pen to draw eyes and mouth on face. Knot fabric strip for scarf and glue to snowman.

3. Glue buttons to corners of small rectangle.

ONE-HOUR DECORATING

Celebrate this holiday season in a very special way — by filling your home with clever handmade decorations. All created in less than one hour, these selections will inspire your crafting talents with fun-to-make pieces for every room in the house! Spruce up your kitchen with a rustic tree-trimmed towel, or accent your mantel with a quick-to-fix tasseled swag. You can also perk up a quiet corner with a holiday button-embellished frame, top your table with elegant place mats, and much more. When you see the exciting ideas in this section, you'll want to start planning a holly-jolly holiday right away!

IN ONLY 30 MINUTES!

Our homey candle has aromatic appeal! It's created by rolling a wax-dipped pillar candle in seasonings you'll find in your pantry. Taking only a half-hour to make, this rustic illuminator is a lovely way to brighten a quiet corner.

AROMATIC SPICED CANDLE
You will need: coffee can, saucepan, newspaper, clear candle wax, black acrylic paint, foam paintbrush, 4" dia. tart pan, Aleene's Weathered Iron Enhancers™ paint, 6"h pillar candle, aluminum foil, spices (we used nutmeg, allspice, and cinnamon), 1" x 18" torn fabric strip, cinnamon stick, and artificial greenery.

1. (**Caution**: Do not melt wax in saucepan placed directly on burner.) Cover work area with newspaper. Place enough wax in can to immerse candle. (Remember that melted wax will rise when candle is immersed.) Place can in saucepan; fill saucepan half full with water. Heat water until wax melts.

2. Thin black paint with a small amount of water. Referring to *Painting Basics* (pg. 104), use foam paintbrush to apply a thin coat of black paint to tart pan; allow to dry slightly.

3. Apply one coat of weathering paint over black paint; allow to dry.

4. Sprinkle desired spices on a 12" square of foil. Holding candle by wick, carefully immerse candle in melted wax; roll in spices. Repeat two more times; allow to harden.

5. Tie fabric strip into a bow around candle. Insert cinnamon stick and greenery behind bow.

*C*ountry charm goes into the making of this fun accent pillow! Torn strips of assorted green fabrics are machine-stitched together over a string and then clipped and gathered to create the shaggy wreath. Just glue the wreath to a ready-made pillow, then add buttons and a contrasting torn-fabric bow for a festive finish!

FABRIC WREATH PILLOW

You will need: $4^1/2$" x 45" torn strips of three coordinating green fabrics, 48" length of string, green thread, 16" square pillow, $2^1/2$" x 26" torn fabric strip for bow, assorted red buttons, and a hot glue gun and glue sticks.

1. Stack green fabric strips together, wrong sides up.

2. Place string along center of fabric strips. Taking care to not stitch through string, use a wide zigzag stitch to sew over string.

3. Making cuts 1" apart, clip fabric up to but not through zigzag stitching on each side of string.

4. Pull string to gather fabric to a 24" length. Tie ends of string together, forming a loop; trim excess string.

5. Center wreath on pillow and glue in place.

6. Tie torn fabric strip into a bow; glue bow to bottom of wreath.

7. Glue buttons to wreath.

The holidays are a whirlwind of activities, and our illuminating snow fellow is just the thing to brighten them! With a little paint, a scrap of flannel fabric, and a candle, you can give heartwarming appeal to an ordinary hurricane globe.

HURRICANE SNOWMAN

You will need: sponge piece; paintbrushes; white, orange, green, and black enamel glass paints; glass hurricane globe; tracing paper; and a 1" x 20" flannel strip.

1. Referring to *Painting Basics* (pg. 104), use sponge piece to stamp white paint on hurricane globe; allow to dry.

2. Trace mitten pattern (pg. 110) onto tracing paper; cut out. Draw around pattern on globe, reversing for opposite hand.

3. Use green paint to paint mittens.

4. Use black paint to paint eyes, mouth, and buttons on snowman and cuffs on mittens. Use white paint to highlight eyes and buttons.

5. Use orange paint to paint nose on snowman; use black paint to add details to nose.

6. For scarf fringe, make clips in ends of flannel strip; tie scarf into a knot around globe.

*O*ur clever lampshade is a crafty way to light up any spot with seasonal greetings. This quick-to-fix little shade is also easy on the pocketbook. You just need a few fabric scraps and felt pieces to add a holly-jolly touch to a plain shade.

FESTIVE LAMPSHADE

You will need: tracing paper, scraps of four assorted fabrics, lampshade, button, black felt, and tacky glue.

1. Trace NOEL letter patterns (pg. 116) onto tracing paper; cut out. Pin patterns to wrong sides of fabric scraps; cut out. Glue letters to lampshade. Glue button to "O."

2. Measure around bottom edge of lampshade; add ¹/₂". Cut a 1"w strip of felt the determined length. Cut one long edge in a zigzag pattern. Glue felt strip to bottom edge of lampshade, overlapping ends ¹/₂".

3. Repeat Step 2 to add felt strip to top edge of lampshade.

*C*raft a colorful decoration to brighten a holiday spot — the tree, the mantel, or an evergreen garland — in less than a half-hour! For this versatile accent, simply glue fanciful heart and snowman cutouts onto a length of festive wooden beads.

SNOWMAN GARLAND

You will need: tracing paper, white and red craft foam, scrap of orange felt, black dimensional paint, four ¹/₂" dia. green buttons, 60" length of wooden bead garland, and a hot glue gun and glue sticks.

1. Trace snowman head, bow tie, nose, and heart patterns (pg. 115) onto tracing paper; cut out. Use patterns to cut three heads, three bow ties, and four hearts from craft foam and three noses from felt.

2. For each snowman, glue bow tie and nose to head. Referring to *Painting*

Basics (pg. 104), use dimensional paint to paint face on snowman.

3. Glue one button to center of each heart.

4. Remove all but twelve beads from garland. Glue back of one heart to string next to twelfth bead. Add twelve more beads to string; glue back of one snowman to string next to twelfth bead. Continue, alternating snowmen and hearts every twelve beads, until all snowmen and hearts are used. Add twelve more beads to string; tie end of string in a knot to secure.

*H*oliday drop-ins will "chill out" in a hurry at the sight of this cool Yule greeting! Dressed in a top hat and bright ribbon scarf, this handsome snowman is a breeze to create from craft foam to dress up a simple pine wreath. Add buttons, snowflakes, red ball ornaments, and sprigs of holly to complete your wintry welcome.

SNOWMAN WREATH

You will need: tracing paper; white, orange, and black craft foam; 4³/₄" length of ¹/₄"w ribbon; one stem of small artificial holly leaves; two ¹/₂" dia. black buttons; three 6¹/₂" dia. snowflake ornaments; three ¹/₂" dia. red buttons; black permanent felt-tip marker; nine small red glass ball ornaments; six large stems of artificial holly leaves with berries; 20" dia. pine wreath; 2 yds. of 1¹/₂"w ribbon; and a hot glue gun and glue sticks.

1. Trace snowman head, hat, and nose patterns (pg. 113) onto tracing paper; cut out. Use patterns to cut one hat from black craft foam, one head from white craft foam, and one nose from orange craft foam.

2. Glue ¹/₄"w ribbon and small holly sprig in place on hat. Glue hat and nose to snowman head. Glue black buttons for eyes to snowman head; use marker to draw mouth.

3. For each snowflake center, remove five small holly leaves from stem. Arrange leaves and glue to center of snowflake. Glue a red button to center of leaves.

4. Arrange large holly stems, snowflake ornaments, glass ball ornaments, and snowman on wreath; glue in place.

5. For scarf, glue ribbon under snowman head and arrange streamers on wreath; glue in place.

6. For scarf fringe, make 1" clips in ribbon ends.

IN ONLY 40 MINUTES!

Our regal tabletop tree combines pretty poinsettias with gilded pinecones, ribbon, and cord. Transmitting graceful harmony from topper to skirt, this tree allows you to exercise your creative talents by artfully arranging a variety of accents among the branches. After gluing the pieces in place, just top the tree with a festive bow and finish off with fabric arranged around the base.

EMBELLISHED TREE

You will need: gold spray paint; pinecones, twigs, and assorted dried plant materials; wire cutters; poinsettia bush with small flowers; 24"h artificial tree; 1 yd. of 1¹/₂"w gold mesh wired ribbon; 1 yd. of gold cord; ¹/₂ yd. of red and green checked fabric; and a hot glue gun and glue sticks.

1. Spray paint pinecones, twigs, and dried plant material; allow to dry.

2. Use wire cutters to remove flowers from poinsettia bush. Arrange flowers, pinecones, twigs, and dried plant materials on tree; glue in place.

3. Tie ribbon into a bow; trim ribbon ends in a "V". Tie cord into a double-loop bow; glue over knot of ribbon bow. Glue bows to top of tree.

4. For tree skirt, arrange fabric around base of tree.

PRETTY POINSETTIA BASKET

IN ONLY 25 MINUTES!

*I*n the blink of an eye, you can create a striking centerpiece! Glue silk flowers and leaves along the edge of a basket and then fill it with natural accents.

POINSETTIA BASKET
You will need: poinsettia bush (ours had 14 flowers), 18" long oblong wicker basket, and a hot glue gun and glue sticks.

1. Remove flowers and leaves from poinsettia bush.

2. Glue flowers and leaves along top edge of basket.

Surprise the bird-watcher in your family with a delightful decorative birdhouse. To save time, the wooden house and star accents are allowed to dry while the tiny tree and evergreen "shingles" are prepared. With all the trims glued in place, the tabletop display is nested in a tuft of Spanish moss.

HOLIDAY BIRDHOUSE

You will need: wood-tone spray; 8"h wooden birdhouse; four $1^{1}/_{2}$"h wooden stars; yellow acrylic paint; paintbrush; $4^{1}/_{2}$" x $6^{1}/_{2}$" rectangles of fabric, poster board, and paper-backed fusible web; tracing paper; wire cutters; artificial pine greenery; black felt-tip pen; floral wire; pencil; small stem of artificial leaves with berries; Spanish moss; twigs; and a hot glue gun and glue sticks.

1. Apply wood-tone spray to birdhouse; paint wooden stars yellow. Allow paint to dry.

2. Referring to *Fusing Basics* (pg. 104), use web to fuse fabric and poster board rectangles together.

3. Trace birdhouse tree pattern (pg. 112) onto tracing paper; cut out. Draw around tree pattern on poster board side of rectangle; cut out.

4. Measure one side of roof from top to bottom. Use wire cutters to cut twelve pieces of pine greenery the determined length. Glue six pieces to each side of roof.

5. Use pen to draw "stitches" on stars. Use wire cutters to cut three 6" lengths of floral wire; wrap around pencil to curl. Glue one wire length to back of each of three stars; glue ends of wires to roof.

6. Glue remaining star to top of tree. Glue tree to front of birdhouse.

7. Use wire cutters to cut three sprigs of leaves and berries from stem. Glue twigs and two sprigs to birdhouse roof; glue remaining sprig to tree.

8. Arrange Spanish moss around base and in openings of birdhouse; glue in place.

*C*lever shortcuts take the real work out of this homey stocking! Begin with a ready-made canvas stocking and fuse on stars made from fabric scraps. Then add a painted wooden star, buttons, and an easy-to-make ruffled cuff. The "stitched" details are simply drawn with a permanent pen!

STAR STOCKING

You will need: 4"h wooden star, gold acrylic paint, paintbrush, paper-backed fusible web, scraps of assorted fabrics for appliqués, canvas stocking, $\frac{1}{8}$ yd. of fabric for ruffle, cotton string, large-eye needle, assorted buttons, black pen, and a hot glue gun and glue sticks.

1. Paint wooden star gold; allow to dry.

2. Referring to *Fusing Basics* (pg. 104), use patterns (pg. 110) to make star appliqués from fabric scraps.

3. Arrange appliqués on stocking front; fuse in place.

4. For ruffle, measure around top of stocking; double this measurement. Tear a piece of fabric 3"w by the determined measurement. Use needle and cotton string to baste $\frac{1}{2}$" from one long edge of fabric piece; pull string to gather ruffle. Adjust gathers evenly to fit around stocking; glue ruffle in place.

5. Use cotton string to tie a triple-loop bow with a 6" tail on each end. Cut a 12" length of string; tie around knot of bow. Glue bow to stocking front below hanging loop; glue a button over knot of bow.

6. Glue wooden star and buttons to stocking.

7. Use pen to draw details around stars and "stitches" around edge of stocking.

*O*ur wintry white Father Christmas
provides a nostalgic focal point for a
Yuletide arrangement. His kindly face
can be cut from gift wrap or an old
greeting card, and he sports a long
beard of curly craft hair. His body
takes shape fast by covering a foam
cone with cotton batting and fur trim.

FATHER CHRISTMAS

You will need: cotton batting, 1/8 yd. of
artificial lamb's wool, tracing paper,
9" x 3 7/8" foam cone, gift wrap or card
with Santa face, 2" length of 1" dia. foam
tube, 3" length of Curly Crepe™ craft
hair, 12" length of floral wire, small piece
of artificial greenery with pinecone, and a
hot glue gun and glue sticks.

1. From batting, cut one 9" x 13 1/2"
piece for coat and one 3" x 10" piece
for sleeves.

2. From lamb's wool, cut one 3 1/2" square
for hood, one 3/4" x 7 1/2" strip for coat
front, one 3/4" x 14" strip for bottom of
coat, and two 3/4" x 3 1/2" strips for cuffs.

3. Trace mitten pattern (pg. 110) onto
tracing paper. Use pattern to cut four
shapes from batting.

4. Overlapping 1/4", glue short edges of
batting piece for coat together, forming a
tube. Place coat over cone. With glued
seam at center front, gather top of coat
around cone and secure with floral wire.

5. Glue 3/4" x 14" wool trim around
bottom of coat. Glue 3/4" x 7 1/2" wool trim
down center front of coat, covering seam.

6. For head, cut face from gift wrap or
card; glue face to foam tube. Cut a 1 1/2"
length of craft hair; glue to face for beard.
Follow craft hair manufacturer's
instructions to fluff beard. Glue head to
top of body.

7. Fold lamb's wool square for hood in
half, wrong sides together. Glue one short
end together. Place over head and glue to
secure.

8. For arms, glue 1 1/2" of each end of
floral wire between two mitten shapes.
Place arm wire along center of batting
piece for sleeves. Place dots of glue over
wire to secure. Glue long edges of sleeves
together. Glue wool trim for cuff around
each sleeve end.

9. Glue center of arms to back of body
just below hat; bend arms to front of
body.

10. Glue greenery to one hand.

CHARMING STOCKING

IN ONLY
25
MINUTES!

Turn on the charm with this elegant gold-trimmed stocking. Braid is glued to a ready-made stocking in a stylized Christmas tree design, and heart-shaped charms serve as "ornaments." Santa is sure to fill this lavish sock with lots of goodies!

HEART CHARM STOCKING

You will need: tracing paper, iron-on transfer pen, ecru stocking, gold braid trim, assorted heart-shaped charms, and a hot glue gun and glue sticks.

1. Use tracing paper and transfer pen to make ribbon tree pattern (pg. 114). Follow pen manufacturer's instructions to transfer pattern to stocking front.

2. Glue gold trim onto stocking over transferred tree design.

3. Arrange charms on tree and glue in place.

HAPPY-GO-LUCKY SNOWMAN

IN ONLY 55 MINUTES!

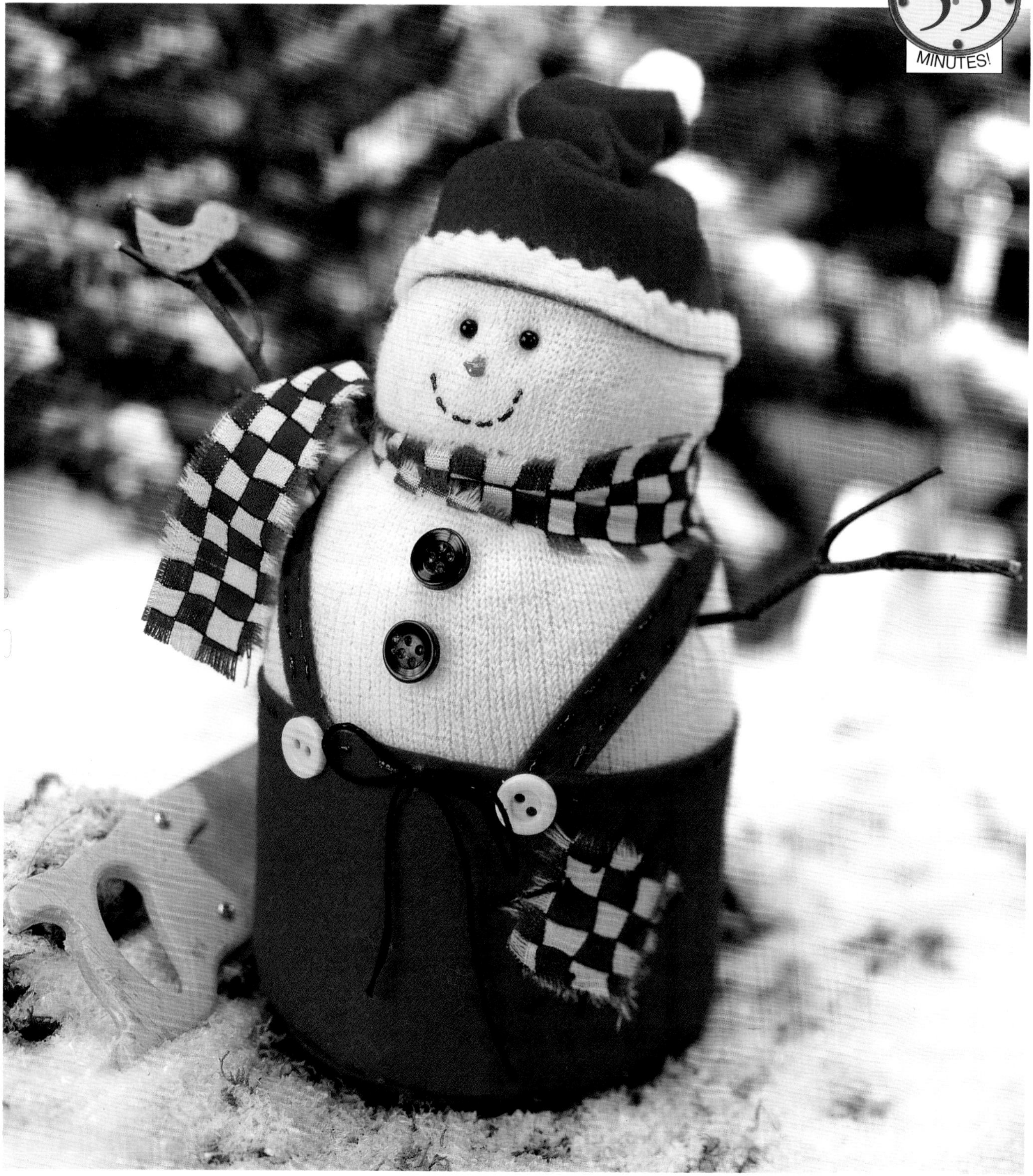

Welcome winter with our happy-go-lucky snowman and his little bird buddy! The jolly fellow is fashioned using sock-covered foam balls, then "dressed" in cheery checked fabric and bright red felt.

BIRD-IN-HAND SNOWMAN

You will need: serrated knife, two 3" dia. foam balls, one 2" dia. foam ball, heavy gauge floral wire, wire cutters, 17" square of polyester batting, rubber band, white sock, tracing paper, $1/2$" x 7" strip of white felt, scrap of yellow felt, black felt-tip pen, pinking shears, $3^1/2$" x $11^1/2$" rectangle of red felt for pants, drawing compass, two $1/4$" x 7" strips of red felt for suspenders, straight pins, 20mm white pom-pom, 1" x 16" torn fabric strip, orange and black dimensional paint, two straight pins with black bead heads, two small black buttons, two small white buttons, two small twigs, black embroidery floss, and a hot glue gun and glue sticks.

1. For base of snowman, use serrated knife to cut one 3" foam ball in half.

2. Stack remaining 3" ball and 2" ball on rounded side of base. Insert floral wire through center of stack; use wire cutters to clip wire end even with top of small ball.

3. Center batting over top of snowman and smooth around head; wrap rubber band around bottom of head. Continue to smooth batting over snowman body. Trim batting even with bottom of base.

4. Pull sock snugly over snowman. Apply glue around edge of base bottom. Press sock into glue; allow to dry. Trim away excess sock.

5. Trace hat and bird patterns (pg. 127) onto tracing paper. Use patterns to cut one hat from red felt and one bird from yellow felt. Use pen to draw details on bird.

6. Overlapping $1/4$", glue straight edges of hat together. For hat trim, use pinking shears to cut along one long edge of $1/2$" x 7" strip of white felt. Matching straight edge of trim to bottom edge of hat, glue trim to hat.

7. Extending felt $1/2$" past bottom edge of base of snowman, wrap felt for pants around snowman body; glue in place. Fold excess fabric under and glue to bottom of base.

8. Use drawing compass and tracing paper to make a 3" dia. pattern; cut one shape from red felt. Glue shape to bottom of snowman.

9. Spacing $1^1/2$" apart, tuck one end of each suspender into front of pants; glue in place. Wrap suspenders over snowman shoulders, crisscrossing at back. Glue remaining ends of suspenders into back of pants.

10. Place hat on snowman head. Use straight pins to hold in place. Fold point of hat over and insert straight pin to scrunch hat down. Glue pom-pom over head of straight pin.

11. For patch, tear a 1" square from one end of fabric strip; glue to pants.

12. Referring to *Painting Basics* (pg. 104), use black paint to paint mouth and draw "stitches" on suspenders, pants, and patch. Apply small dots of orange paint for snowman nose and bird beak. For eyes, insert beaded straight pins into head.

13. Glue black buttons to snowman chest, and white buttons below front suspenders.

14. For arms, insert ends of twigs into sides of snowman body. Glue bird to one arm.

15. Tie scarf around snowman neck. Tie a 10" length of embroidery floss into a bow; glue to front of pants.

You can bring the enticing scent of country spice into your home with our clove-studded candles. These stunning wax creations are a breeze to make by embellishing pillar candles with cloves, pinecones, and anise stars.

CLOVE-STUDDED CANDLES

You will need: gold spray paint, two 3½" dia. jar lids, drawing compass, corrugated cardboard, black pen, disposable lighter, whole cloves, whole anise stars, preserved pine greenery, miniature pinecones, metallic gold acrylic paint, small paintbrush, and a hot glue gun and glue sticks.

For tall candle, you will also need: 3"dia. x 6"h white candle and pinecone roses.

For short candle, you will also need: 3"dia. x 3"h white candle.

1. Apply one coat of gold spray paint to jar lids; allow to dry.

2. Use compass to draw two 4½" dia. circles on cardboard; cut out.

3. Center one jar lid right side up on each cardboard circle; draw around lid on cardboard. Apply glue to drawn circle; press rim of lid into glue. Place one candle in each jar lid and glue in place; allow to dry.

4. Use pen to place dots on candles for clove placement. Heat point of compass over flame of lighter and insert point into each dot to melt wax slightly.

5. Trim each clove stem so that ⅛" of stem remains. Place a dot of glue on end of each stem, then quickly insert clove into hole in candle.

6. For each candle, cut several 4" lengths of greenery. Glue greenery around edge of cardboard circle, overlapping as needed.

7. For tall candle, glue three pinecone roses and two miniature pinecones onto greenery at base of candle. Use gold acrylic paint to highlight cloves, roses, and pinecones.

8. For short candle, glue six anise stars and six miniature pinecones onto greenery at base of candle. Use gold acrylic paint to highlight anise stars, pinecones, and cloves.

*R*esembling an old-fashioned wool rug, this provincial banner evokes the warmth of home. The simple wish, crafted from fabric scraps, is easily created using a reverse appliqué technique. Basic embroidery, a holly accent, and a twig hanger complete the homey look.

NOEL BANNER
You will need: tracing paper, two black felt pieces, poster board, paper-backed fusible web, small sharp scissors, four 1¹/₂" x 3" rectangles of assorted fabrics, gold and black embroidery floss, scrap of green felt, buttons, 12" long twig, and a hot glue gun and glue sticks.

1. Referring to *Making Patterns* (pg. 104), trace banner pattern (pg. 116) onto tracing paper. Use pattern to cut banner from black felt.

2. Cut one 5¹/₂" x 7¹/₄" rectangle each from poster board, fusible web, and black felt.

3. Referring to *Fusing Basics* (pg. 104), center fusible web rectangle over NOEL pattern (pg. 116) and trace letters onto paper side of web. Center and fuse to wrong side of banner; do not remove paper backing. Use small sharp scissors to carefully cut out letters. Remove paper backing and save for use in Step 4.

4. Place right side of one fabric rectangle over each cut-out letter on web side of banner. Place paper backing over fabric pieces and banner; fuse fabric rectangles in place. Remove paper backing.

5. Referring to *Embroidery Stitches* (pg. 105), use three strands of gold floss to work Running Stitch around edge of fusible web rectangle.

6. Trace leaf pattern (pg. 116) onto tracing paper; cut out. Use pattern to cut two leaves from green felt. Use three strands of black floss to work Running Stitch to stitch leaves to corner of banner.

7. Use black floss to sew a button to each corner of banner.

8. Place poster board rectangle over back of banner; fuse to secure.

9. For hanging tabs, cut two ¹/₂" x 4" strips from black felt. Fold each strip in half; glue ends of tabs to top back of banner.

10. Glue black felt rectangle over poster board.

11. Insert twig through hanging tabs.

GINGER GIRL STOCKING

IN ONLY 30 MINUTES!

*T*his sweet stocking will be ready to hold lots of Santa's goodies on Christmas Eve! We used a ready-made stocking to save time. The cheery motifs are quickly glued in place, along with the contrasting buttons and rickrack.

GINGER GIRL STOCKING

You will need: 14" canvas stocking, red jumbo rickrack, tracing paper, craft knife, yellow foam meat tray, floral wood-tone spray, red felt piece, two 5mm white pom-poms, white baby rickrack, nine white buttons, 12" length of 1"w grosgrain ribbon, and tacky glue.

1. Measure around top and toe of stocking; cut a length of jumbo rickrack for each measurement. Glue each rickrack length to stocking.

2. Trace body, cheek, foot, and heart patterns (pg. 117) onto tracing paper; cut out. Use craft knife to cut one body shape from foam tray. Cut two each of cheek and foot shapes and one heart from felt.

3. Spray body with wood-tone spray; allow to dry. Glue felt cutouts and pom-poms for eyes to body.

4. Trimming to fit, glue white rickrack across arms and legs, along neck, and around top of head. Glue a small piece of white rickrack to face for mouth.

5. Glue ginger girl to stocking.

6. Glue buttons to ginger girl and stocking.

7. Tie ribbon into a bow; glue to head.

*B*ring an extra measure of cheer to your home with this "merry" greeting. It's created with purchased wooden letters that are painted and glued inside star-shaped cookie cutters. Torn-fabric bows tie it all together.

"BE MERRY" STARS

You will need: red and green acrylic paint, paintbrushes, 1³/₄"h wooden letter cutouts to spell BE MERRY, white dimensional paint, seven 1" x 7" torn fabric strips, seven 3"w star-shaped metal cookie cutters, and a hot glue gun and glue sticks.

1. Apply one coat of red paint to letters that spell the word MERRY; allow to dry.

2. Apply one coat of green paint to letters that spell the word BE; allow to dry.

3. Referring to *Painting Basics* (pg. 104), use dimensional paint to apply dots to all letters.

4. Use torn fabric strips to tie five cookie cutters together and to tie a bow to cookie cutter at each end. Tie remaining two cookie cutters together. Insert letters into cookie cutters to spell words; glue in place.

59

Relatives and friends will be delighted with this quilt-look wall hanging that's touched with love. Little ones will enjoy "lending a hand" to make the dated banner, which features the child's name and handprint. The no-sew accent is quick to fuse together.

HANDPRINT WALL HANGING

You will need: paper-backed fusible web, 7¹/₄" fabric square, 8¹/₂" fabric square, 9" square of cotton batting, 9" fabric square, scraps of coordinating fabric for appliqués, black felt-tip pen, green floral wire, pencil, buttons, and a hot glue gun and glue sticks.

1. For handprint appliqué, draw around child's hand on paper side of fusible web. Referring to *Fusing Basics* (pg. 104), fuse web to wrong side of fabric scrap; cut out handprint.

2. Use patterns (pg. 116) to make one heart appliqué and one banner appliqué. Make four matching 1" square appliqués (for corners) from fabric scraps.

3. Fuse web to wrong side of a 2¹/₂" x 6" piece of fabric; do not remove paper backing. Fuse banner to right side of fused fabric. Trim fabric ¹/₄" from outside edge of appliqué.

4. Fuse web to wrong side of 7¹/₄", 8¹/₂", and 9" squares. Do not remove paper.

5. For front of wall hanging, center 7¹/₄" square on right side of 8¹/₂" square and fuse in place.

6. Arrange hand, heart, banner, and corner appliqués on wall hanging front and fuse in place.

7. For back of wall hanging, fuse batting square and 9" fabric square together.

8. Center wall hanging front on back piece and fuse in place. Trim back piece ¹/₈" outside edge of front.

9. Use pen to write child's name and draw border designs on banner.

10. Cut a 15" length of floral wire. Wrap center 11" of wire around pencil to curl.

Insert ends of wire through front of wall hanging and bend ends to back.

11. Cut a ³/₄" x 12" strip of fabric; tie into a bow. Glue two buttons over knot of bow; glue bow to center of wire.

12. Glue buttons to wall hanging front.

"BERRY" CUTE ANGEL

No one will ever guess this Christmas cutie was created in only minutes! To craft a dress for a purchased muslin doll, join the edges of your fabric with an easy running stitch, then gather one edge to form the neckline. Ready-made pieces, such as the hat and basket, are great accessories. Raffia wings add heavenly final touches.

CHRISTMAS BERRY ANGEL

You will need: tracing paper, iron-on transfer pen, black pen, red colored pencil, 18"h muslin doll, 12¹⁄₂" x 44" torn rectangle of red print fabric, needle, thread to match fabric, ³⁄₄" x 26" torn fabric strip, one ³⁄₄" dia. button, 6" dia. sinamay hat, preserved cedar, wire cutters, one stem of artificial berries with leaves, natural raffia, small straw basket, and a hot glue gun and glue sticks.

1. Using tracing paper and transfer pen, follow pen manufacturer's instructions to transfer doll face pattern (pg. 112) to doll.

2. Use black pen to draw over face on doll. Use red pencil to color cheeks and lips.

3. For dress, overlap short ends of red fabric ¹⁄₂". Referring to *Embroidery Stitches* (pg. 105), use a Running Stitch to sew edges together, forming a tube. Baste around one raw edge of tube; pull threads to gather. Place dress on doll, adjusting gathers to fit at neck. Knot and trim thread ends. For sleeves, cut a slit in each side of dress; place arms through slits.

4. Center torn fabric strip at back of neck and wrap around doll, crisscrossing in front. Tie ends of fabric strip at back of doll. Glue button over crossed fabric strip at front of dress.

5. For hatband, glue several sprigs of cedar around hat. Use wire cutters to cut one sprig of berries; glue sprig to hatband. Glue hat to head.

6. For wings, cut several 36" lengths of raffia; tie into a bow. Glue wings to back of doll.

7. Use wire cutters to cut a few sprigs of berries; glue sprigs inside basket.

8. Place basket on arm; glue hands together to keep basket in place.

RUSTIC KITCHEN TOWEL

IN ONLY **35** *MINUTES!*

O̶ur Christmas tree towel gets its charming homespun look from a mixture of fabric scraps. Fusible web appliqués and machine stitching make this towel surprisingly quick to assemble.

CHRISTMAS TREE KITCHEN TOWEL
You will need: 7" x 10" and 6" x 9" fabric rectangles, paper-backed fusible web, scraps of assorted fabrics for appliqués, clear nylon thread, kitchen towel, red embroidery floss, and four $^1/_2$" dia. red buttons.

1. Press edges of both fabric rectangles $^1/_2$" to wrong side. Center smaller rectangle on larger rectangle; topstitch in place along pressed edges.

2. Referring to *Fusing Basics* (pg. 104), use tree bottom, tree top, tree trunk, and tree topper patterns (pg. 118) to make appliqués from fabric scraps. Arrange appliqués on center of fabric rectangles and fuse in place. Use a narrow zigzag stitch and clear nylon thread to stitch over edges of appliqués.

3. Position rectangle on towel; topstitch in place along outer edges.

4. Use embroidery floss to sew one button to each corner of large rectangle.

*S*weet-smelling spices, a
nostalgic greeting card, and
perky checked fabric transform
an ordinary basket into a pretty
decoration. Equipped with a hot
glue gun and pinking shears, you
can assemble this lovely container
in 30 minutes flat!

RUSTIC BASKET
You will need: pinking shears; 5" squares
of checked fabric, paper-backed fusible
web, and poster board; woven basket at

least 6¹/₄"h from bottom to rim; Christmas
card; ⁵/₈"w green grosgrain ribbon; two
whole anise stars; cinnamon sticks;
miniature pinecones; dried apple slice;
dried cranberries; sprig of artificial pine
greenery; and a hot glue gun and
glue sticks.

1. Referring to *Fusing Basics* (pg. 104),
use web to fuse fabric and poster board
together. Pink edges of fused square.

2. Cut desired motif from card. Center
motif on fabric square; glue in place.
Center square on front of basket; glue
in place.

3. Measure around rim of basket; add 1".
Cut a length of ribbon the determined
measurement. Overlapping ends at center
front of basket, glue ribbon around rim.
Cut a 30" length of ribbon. Tie ribbon into
a double-loop bow and glue to ribbon at
front of basket. Glue one anise star to
knot of bow.

4. Arrange remaining anise star, dried
fruit, cinnamon sticks, pinecones, and
greenery over one corner of fabric
square; glue in place.

63

COUNTRY STOCKING GARLAND

IN ONLY 45 MINUTES!

Infant socks and fabric scraps provide an easy way to trim this star-studded string. Patches fused to the tea-dyed "stockings" and cinnamon sticks laced onto the garland add to the country appeal.

STOCKING SWAG

You will need: paper-backed fusible web, scraps of assorted fabrics, infant-size white socks, tea dye bath, cinnamon sticks, black medium-point marker, 2" dia. wooden star cutouts, $3/4$" dia. green buttons, craft wire, twelve 15mm red wooden beads, mini clothespins, and a hot glue gun and glue sticks.

1. Referring to *Fusing Basics* (pg. 104), use heel and toe patterns (pg. 117) to make appliqués. Arrange appliqués on socks and fuse in place.

2. Follow dye manufacturer's instructions to dye socks.

3. Cut six 4" lengths from cinnamon sticks.

4. Tear eighteen 1" x 8" strips from assorted fabrics. Knot three strips around center of each cinnamon stick.

5. Use marker to draw "stitches" on stars. Glue one button to center of each star; glue one star to center of each cinnamon stick.

6. Cut a 60" length of craft wire. Arrange swag as follows: one bead, one cinnamon stick, one bead; repeat order until all cinnamon sticks and beads are used, ending with one bead. Use a clothespin to attach each sock to wire between two beads.

64

*N*ovelty buttons, painted in bright Christmasy hues, add a festive touch to a plain wooden frame. Just thread the stars, hearts, and trees onto a length of embroidery floss and glue them around the edges. It's a great spot to show off a photo of the star of the family!

BUTTON FRAME

You will need: small wooden star, heart, and tree buttons; yellow, red, and green acrylic paint; paintbrushes; white embroidery floss; needle; 5" x 7" wooden frame; and glue.

1. Paint buttons desired colors; allow to dry.

2. Thread buttons onto a 36" length of floss; knot ends of floss together.

3. Arrange buttons around frame and glue in place.

QUICK PILLOW WRAP

*Y*ou can add luster to a velvet
pillow in less time than it takes Santa
to settle his sleigh on your rooftop!
Sew two fabric napkins together,
arrange them around the pillow,
gather the ends with a rubber band,
and finish with a tasseled gold cord!

HOLIDAY PILLOW
You will need: two 18" square metallic
gold cloth napkins, 12" x 16" green velvet
pillow, rubber band, and a 13" long gold
cord with tasseled ends.

1. Using a ¹/₄" seam allowance, sew
napkins together along one edge.

2. Wrap napkins around pillow
and gather ends with a rubber band;
adjust gathers.

3. Tie cord around napkin ends,
covering rubber band.

IN ONLY
10
MINUTES!

*O*ur no-sew tasseled holiday scarf is a tasteful highlight for a handsome mantelpiece. In only half an hour, you can transform pretty cloth napkins into an eye-catching accent.

CHRISTMAS MANTEL SCARF

You will need: one 17" square of paper-backed fusible web, three 17" square fabric Christmas napkins, three gold tassels, and a hot glue gun and glue sticks.

1. Cut an 8¹/₂" square from one corner of fusible web. Cut 8¹/₂" square in half diagonally, making two triangles.

2. Referring to *Fusing Basics* (pg. 104), fuse a web triangle to wrong side of one corner (top) of each of two napkins. For center piece of mantel scarf, fuse remaining web piece to remaining napkin. (This will leave an 8¹/₂" square of this napkin free of web.)

3. Arrange napkins wrong side up as shown in Fig. 1, positioning fused sections at top of scarf.

Fig. 1

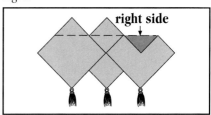

right side

4. Fold (indicated by dotted line) top corners to wrong side of scarf and fuse in place.

5. Glue hanging loop of one tassel to wrong side of each lower point of mantel scarf.

POINSETTIA TOPIARY BANNER

Our bright and cheery banner is a colorful reminder of this joyous season. Vibrant silk poinsettia petals and leaves are fused to a canvas banner, then fabric pieces are added to create the flowerpot and topiary stem.

YULETIDE BANNER

You will need: 19³/₄" x 27¹/₂" canvas banner with dowel and dowel caps, white spray paint, 23" long gold cord with tasseled ends, aluminum foil, paper-backed fusible web, silk poinsettia bush with five flowers, ¹/₄ yd. of Christmas fabric, 1"w fusible web tape, ³/₄" x 6" rectangle of green fabric, 20" length of 2¹/₂"w gold wired ribbon, gold dimensional paint, and a hot glue gun and glue sticks.

Note: Refer to *Fusing Basics* (pg. 104) for Steps 2 through 6, following Foil Method for Step 3.

1. Use spray paint to paint dowel and dowel caps; allow to dry.

2. Cut two 1" x 27¹/₂" and two 1" x 19³/₄" strips of Christmas fabric. Fuse web tape to wrong side of each strip. Arrange strips along edges of banner; fuse in place.

3. Remove leaves and petals from poinsettia bush. Fuse web to wrong sides of petals and leaves to make appliqués.

4. Use pattern (pg. 119) to make one flowerpot appliqué from Christmas fabric.

5. For stem appliqué, fuse web tape to wrong side of green fabric.

6. Arrange poinsettia, flowerpot, and stem appliqués on banner and fuse in place.

7. Tie ribbon into a bow; glue to top of flowerpot.

8. Referring to *Painting Basics* (pg. 104), use dimensional paint to apply dots at flower centers.

9. Tie one end of gold cord to each end of dowel.

IN ONLY
25
MINUTES!

*L*ooking for an elegant addition to your holiday table? Then this quick project is for you! Silk flower petals and leaves are removed from the stems and fused onto the corner of an ordinary place mat. Gold dimensional paint finishes the project with sparkle. Craft several to make a festive setting for your dinner guests.

POINSETTIA PLACE MAT

You will need: one white silk poinsettia with eight to ten petals, aluminum foil, paper-backed fusible web, red fabric place mat, and gold glitter dimensional paint.

1. Remove leaves and petals from poinsettia stem.

2. Referring to *Fusing Basics* (pg. 104), follow Foil Method to fuse web to wrong sides of poinsettia petals and leaves for appliqués.

3. Arrange appliqués on one corner of place mat; fuse in place.

4. Referring to *Painting Basics* (pg. 104), paint over edges of each appliqué; paint detail lines on petals and leaves.

69

APPEALING SNOW LADY

*O*ur appealing, one-of-a-kind snow lady tree is an attention-getting decoration indoors or out! Her charming personality is easy to create when you start with a flocked pine tree. Simply top the tree with a stuffed trash bag "head" sporting craft foam facial features and finish it off with mittened dowel-rod "arms" and a scarf!

SNOW LADY TREE

You will need: large white trash bag; large bag of polyester fiberfill; large rubber band; tracing paper; yellow, orange, pink, blue, and black craft foam; craft knife; 1$^1/_2$ yds. of 1$^1/_2$"w red wired ribbon; three $^3/_8$" dia. dowel rods; 36"h flocked pine tree; 6" x 44" torn strip of fabric for scarf; and craft glue.

1. For head, fill trash bag with polyester fiberfill. Secure opening with rubber band. Tie ribbon into a bow around opening, covering rubber band; trim ends.

2. Trace eye, nose, cheek, mouth, cuff and mitten, patterns (pgs. 120 and 121) onto tracing paper; cut out. Referring to photo for colors, use patterns and craft knife to cut shapes from craft foam.

3. Glue eyes, nose, cheeks, and mouth to head; allow to dry. Glue a mitten and cuff to one end of each of two dowel rods; allow to dry.

4. Insert one end of remaining dowel into bottom of head. Slide opposite end of dowel into top center of tree. Position arms in sides of tree.

5. Loosely knot strip of fabric for scarf around dowel below head.

SPICY FEATHER TREE

*B*ring Christmas to the kitchen when you stir up this spicy feather tree! The tree is created using a wooden spoon for a trunk, and it's trimmed with berries, dried orange slices, and star anise. A clay pot topped with wood excelsior serves as the base.

FRAGRANT SPOON TREE

You will need: 13" long wooden spoon, wood-tone spray, cinnamon stick, 1" x 18" strip of torn fabric, wire cutters, artificial pine greenery, 4" wooden star cutout, 5" fabric square, dried orange slices, stem of artificial berries, whole star anise, serrated knife, 2" square of floral foam, 4" clay pot, wood excelsior, and a hot glue gun and glue sticks.

1. Apply one coat of wood-tone spray to spoon; allow to dry.

2. Break cinnamon stick in half; glue halves to front of pot. Wrap fabric strip around pot and tie into a bow over cinnamon sticks.

3. For "tree," use wire cutters to cut two 4", two 3", three 2", and one 1" length of pine greenery. Spacing 1^1/$_2$" apart and beginning 3" from bottom of spoon handle, glue greenery to spoon, using smaller lengths toward bowl of spoon.

4. Place wooden star on wrong side of fabric square. Draw around star; cut out shape. Glue fabric star to wooden star; glue wooden star to bowl of spoon.

5. Cut orange slices in half. Remove eight berries from stem. Arrange orange slice halves, anise stars, and berries on tree; glue in place.

6. Place floral foam in pot. Insert spoon handle into foam; glue excelsior over surface of foam.

ONE-HOUR TREE TRIMMING

*H*oliday spirits soar as soon as we trim the Christmas tree! In this section, we offer fast-to-fix projects to cover your tree in style, from tree topper to skirt and all in between. Sprinkle your tree with Santas, stars, and snowmen to create an air of elegance, rustic charm, or playfulness. You'll find shiny glass ornaments accented with unique designs and a precious photo surrounded by a golden circle of buttons. You can also whip up some bright three-dimensional stars or a whimsical snowman crafted from a washcloth. Make this the year to add pizzazz to your tree with the clever, quickly assembled tree-trimmers on the following pages!

IN ONLY
45
MINUTES!

With a wave of his wand, this jolly old elf will bring holiday magic to your Christmas tree! Our primitive Santa is simple to make using padded fabric-covered bristol board and painted craft sticks. He's sure to make the holidays special.

MAGIC SANTA ORNAMENT

You will need: tracing paper; drawing compass; $4^1/2$" squares of bristol board and batting; $5/8$" dia. button; $4^1/2$" length of $3/8$"w black grosgrain ribbon; paintbrush; black paint; jumbo craft stick; scraps of two red fabrics, white felt, and red felt; white thread; $3/8$" dia. button; 3"w wooden heart cutout; black pen; red colored pencil; $1^1/2$"w wooden star cutout; wooden craft pick; and a hot glue gun and glue sticks.

1. For Santa body, use tracing paper and compass to make $3^1/2$" dia. and $4^1/2$" dia. circle patterns. Use $3^1/2$" pattern to cut one circle each from bristol board and batting. Glue batting circle to bristol board circle.

2. Use $4^1/2$" pattern to cut circle from one red fabric. Center glued circles batting side down on wrong side of fabric circle. Wrap fabric edges to back of circle; glue in place.

3. For belt and buckle, sew larger button to center of ribbon. Center and glue ribbon to body, wrapping ends to back.

4. Use $3^1/2$" pattern to cut one circle from red felt; glue over back of body.

5. For arms, paint ends of craft stick black; allow to dry. For sleeves, cut a 2" x 4" rectangle from remaining red fabric; center and glue around craft stick. For cuffs, cut two $1/2$" x $2^1/4$" strips of white felt; glue one strip around craft stick at end of each sleeve.

6. Trace beard and hat patterns (pg. 120) onto tracing paper. Use patterns to cut hat from red felt and beard from white felt.

7. With heart cutout upside down, wrap hat around point, overlapping at back; glue in place. For hatband, cut a $1/4$" x 3" strip of white felt; glue to bottom of hat, overlapping ends at back. Sew small button to top of hat.

8. Use pen to draw eyes and red pencil to color cheeks. Glue beard just below center of cheeks.

9. Center head on arms; glue in place. Center arms on top front of body; glue in place. Glue wooden star to craft pick; glue craft pick to hand.

SIMPLE STARS

*C*reate a galaxy of heavenly
ornaments using painted wooden
stars! Corrugated cardboard
accented with colorful buttons adds
a textured touch to the bright pieces.

WOODEN STAR ORNAMENTS

For each ornament, you will need:
5" wooden star, acrylic paint, paintbrush,
corrugated craft cardboard, gold craft
wire, pencil, assorted buttons, and glue.

1. Paint star desired color; allow to dry.

2. Draw around wooden star on
cardboard. Cut out cardboard star ¹/₄"
inside drawn line. Center cardboard star,
corrugated side up, on wooden star; glue
in place.

3. Cut a 15" length of craft wire. Wrap 3"
of each end of wire around pencil to curl.

4. Thread each end of wire through a
button; twist at back of button to secure.
Bend wire into an arc and glue to back
of star.

5. Glue assorted buttons to front of
ornament.

GOOD-AS-GOLD ORNAMENT

IN ONLY 8 MINUTES!

*T*his glimmering bauble is as good as gold! And it's so quick to make, you can craft one for everyone you know. Simply wrap a matte-finish ornament with shiny trim, top it with a silk poinsettia, and attach a gold cord hanger.

LUSTROUS GOLD ORNAMENT
You will need: gold silk poinsettia, 3½" dia. gold matte-finish ornament, 10" length of ⅝"w gold trim, 8" length of gold cord, and a hot glue gun and glue sticks.

1. Remove petals, leaves, and flower center from poinsettia.

2. Glue leaves, then petals around top of ornament.

3. Glue trim around center of ornament.

4. Thread flower center through ornament hanger and glue in place.

5. Thread cord through hanger; knot ends together.

*T*his stunning tree topper will capture the attention of star-gazers! Gilded trim outlines the shimmering brocade patchwork, and a golden cord bow provides an elegant finish.

BROCADE STAR TREE TOPPER

You will need: tracing paper, poster board, paper-backed fusible web, scraps of five assorted brocade lamé fabrics, $1^1/_3$ yds. of $^3/_8$"w gold trim, 36" long gold cord with tasseled ends, 3" length of floral wire, and a hot glue gun and glue sticks.

1. Referring to *Making Patterns* (pg. 104), trace star pattern (pg. 119) onto tracing paper; cut out. Use pattern to cut one star from poster board.

2. Referring to *Fusing Basics* (pg. 104), use pattern to make five star segment appliqués from fabrics. Arrange appliqués on poster board star; fuse in place.

3. Glue gold trim around all edges of appliqués.

4. Tie cord into a double bow; glue bow to center of star.

5. For hanger, bend floral wire to form a loop; glue loop to back of star.

77

*N*eed some quick and easy tree-trimmers to share with co-workers or neighbors? This homespun ornament is the perfect project! Just wrap fabric around a plastic foam ball, gather with ribbon, and add a starry accent.

FABRIC-COVERED ORNAMENT

You will need: paintbrush, yellow acrylic paint, two 4"w wooden star cutouts, black pen, drawing compass, newspaper, 12" square of fabric, 3" dia. foam ball, rubber band, 1 yd. of ¼"w green ribbon, floral pin, and a hot glue gun and glue sticks.

1. Apply one coat of paint to each star; allow to dry.

2. Use compass to make a 12" circle pattern from newspaper. Use pattern to cut one shape from fabric square.

3. Center foam ball on wrong side of fabric circle. Gather edges of fabric around foam ball. Wrap rubber band around gathers to secure; adjust gathers.

4. Cut an 18" length of ribbon; tie into a bow around gathers, covering rubber band.

5. Cut a 14" length of ribbon; fold in half. Matching star edges, glue folded ribbon between stars, leaving a 2" loop at top for hanger. Use pen to draw "stitches" around edges of each star.

6. Tie remaining ends of ribbon into a knot. Insert floral pen through knot and into top of ornament.

*W*ith her cute button face, this little angel is sure to bring a country air to your tree! Her simple attire is made of felt and buttons, and her freckled face is easy to draw using markers. Yarn doll hair crowns her with curls, and chenille stem "wings" are ready to take flight.

FRECKLED ANGEL ORNAMENT

You will need: $3^1/_2$" x 4" pieces of poster board, ecru felt, and paper-backed fusible web; tracing paper; scraps of gold felt and muslin; $1^1/_8$" dia. covered button kit; brown and black markers; brown curly yarn doll hair; two brown chenille stems; 6" length of gold craft wire; six assorted brown buttons; 4" length of floral wire; gold embroidery floss; and a hot glue gun and glue sticks.

1. Following manufacturer's instructions, use web to fuse felt to poster board.

2. Trace small angel body and star patterns (pg. 117) onto tracing paper; cut out. Use pattern to cut angel from fused rectangle.

3. Use pattern to cut one star from gold felt; glue to felt side of angel body.

4. For angel head, follow manufacturer's instructions to cover button with muslin. Use markers to draw face and freckles.

5. Cut a small amount of curly yarn and glue to top of head. Glue head to angel body.

6. For wings, cut two 8" lengths of chenille stems. Bend stems into wing shapes; glue to back of ornament.

7. For halo, bend craft wire into a circle; twist ends together. Glue halo to back of head.

8. Glue buttons to front of ornament.

9. For hanger, bend floral wire into a hook; glue to back of ornament.

10. Cut two 12" lengths of embroidery floss. Place lengths together; tie into a bow. Glue bow to angel under chin.

79

JOLLY SANTA BELL

*R*ing in the holidays with an ornament fashioned after everyone's favorite gift-giver! Transfer paper makes it a cinch to paint Santa's jolly face onto a papier-mâché bell. A fluffy pom-pom tops his hat.

SANTA BELL ORNAMENT

You will need: white, flesh, cream, pink, red, very light grey, and black acrylic paint; paintbrushes; tracing paper; transfer paper; stylus; 4"h papier-mâché bell ornament; black pen; 20mm pom-pom; and craft glue.

1. Paint ornament white; allow to dry.

2. Trace Santa face pattern (pg. 118) onto tracing paper. Use stylus and transfer paper to transfer pattern to bell. Extend hat and hat trim lines around back of ornament.

3. Using transferred lines as a guide, paint face flesh and cap and mouth red. Using a stamping motion, paint hat trim cream. Use pink paint to paint nose, cheek lines, and lips. Use very light grey paint to shade area below mustache. Allow to dry.

4. Use black pen to draw eyes and to add detail lines. Use white paint to highlight eyes, nose, and cheeks; paint eyebrows; and paint dots on hat.

5. Glue pom-pom to top of ornament; allow to dry.

Making this cheery ornament is child's play! Wooden alphabet blocks and beads are laced onto craft wire, which is shaped into a ring. Berry sprigs and a wooden star give the hanger festive charm.

CIRCLE OF JOY ORNAMENT
You will need: craft drill, wooden alphabet blocks to spell JOY, wire cutters, black craft wire, red and green wooden beads, pencil, holly berry sprigs, 2"w wooden star, and a hot glue gun and glue sticks.

1. Use craft drill to drill a hole horizontally through center of each block.

2. Use wire cutters to cut a 28" length of craft wire. Thread wire through one red and one green bead, through Y block, through one green bead, through O block, through one green bead, through J block, and through one green and one red bead.

3. Bend wire into a circle. Cross wires 5" from ends; twist wires together at top of circle. Wrap wire ends around pencil to curl.

4. Cut a 12" length of wire; bend to form hanging loop. Attach loop to top of circle by twisting wires together at bottom of loop; curl ends.

5. Wrap ends of berry sprigs around base of loop; glue in place. Glue blocks in place on wire.

6. Glue wooden star over base of hanging loop.

81

CARDINAL'S PERCH

A *"snowcapped" pinecone makes a perfect perch for this vibrant feathered friend! A sprig of wintertime berries finishes the ornament with Yuletide spirit — in only seven minutes!*

CARDINAL ORNAMENT

You will need: Delta Fantasy Snow™, large pinecone, 12" length of ¹/₈"w red ribbon, artificial cardinal, small sprig of white artificial berries, and craft glue.

1. For hanger, fold ribbon in half, forming a loop. Tie a knot 2" from fold; glue ribbon ends under one wing of bird.

2. Follow manufacturer's instructions to apply snow to top of pinecone, leaving a 1" dia. opening at center top of pinecone.

3. Glue bird onto snow, covering opening. Glue berry sprig to snow. Allow to dry.

*S*hare a touch of country charm with these rustic rag ball ornaments. They're super-fast to create using strips of torn fabric wrapped over foam balls. Buttons from your stash top off the natural raffia bows.

RAG BALL ORNAMENTS

For each ornament, you will need: 3" dia. foam ball, ⅛ yd. of fabric, natural raffia, button, and a hot glue gun and glue sticks.

1. Tear seven 1¼" x 9" strips of fabric; press.

2. Overlapping long edges and twisting fabric at bottom of ball, wrap six fabric strips around ball. Glue ends of strips in place at top of ball; allow to dry.

3. For ornament hanger, glue ends of remaining fabric strip together, forming a loop. Glue to top of ornament.

4. Cut several 4" lengths of raffia; use one length of raffia to tie remaining lengths together at center. Glue to hanger.

5. Glue button over raffia.

IN ONLY
20
MINUTES!

Here's a great way to dress up ordinary glass baubles. Simply spray assorted trims with adhesive and apply them to the ornaments as you please. Your creativity is what makes these accents unique!

ELEGANT ORNAMENTS
For each ornament, you will need: assorted gold, silver, and ecru trims; newspaper; spray adhesive; 3" dia. gold glass ornament; and a 7" length of gold cord.

1. Cut trims into 9¹/₂" lengths.

2. Place trims on newspaper wrong side up; spray with adhesive.

3. Wrap trims around ornament as desired, trimming ends as necessary.

4. Thread cord through hanger; knot ends together.

*B*rilliant baubles of gold lamé adorn this easy-to-decorate skirt. Any plain purchased tree skirt can be used as a base for the gilded motifs. No-sew fusing makes them simple to attach. Glue on touches of ribbon and braid for extra special embellishments.

ELEGANT TREE SKIRT

You will need: ecru tree skirt, paper-backed fusible web, ¼ yd. of gold lamé fabric, 1"w fusible web tape, aluminum foil, 1¼"w gold trim, ⅜"w gold trim, and 1½ yds. of ⅝"w gold mesh ribbon.

1. Referring to *Fusing Basics* (pg. 104), use patterns (pgs. 122) to make one ornament B and two ornament A appliqués from gold lamé.

2. Arrange appliqués on tree skirt and fuse in place.

3. Referring to *Fusing Basics* (pg. 104), follow Foil Method to fuse web tape to

wrong side of 1¼"w gold trim. Cut trim into lengths to fit across ornaments. Arrange trim on ornaments and fuse in place.

4. Measure distances from inner edge of tree skirt to top of each ornament; cut a length of ⅜"w trim for each of the determined measurements. Fuse web tape to wrong side of trims; arrange on tree skirt and fuse in place.

5. Cut three 18" lengths of gold mesh ribbon. Tie each length into a bow and glue one bow to top of each ornament.

*O*ur little Santa bear looks so sweet nestled in a decorated teacup! The tiny packages that fill his arms are crafted by wrapping plastic foam pieces with scraps of festive felt.

TEACUP BEAR

You will need: tracing paper; scraps of white, red, and green felt; 10mm white pom-pom; two small rectangles of plastic foam; 18" length of ⅛"w red ribbon; 6" length of ⅛"w green ribbon; white teacup; red and green paint pens; 6" tall stuffed bear, 8" length of heavy gauge floral wire; and a hot glue gun and glue sticks.

1. Trace bear hat and bear hat trim patterns (pg. 126) onto tracing paper; cut out. Use patterns to cut one hat from red felt and one hat trim from white felt. Overlap short edges of hat and glue in place, trimming as necessary. Glue hat trim around bottom of hat. Scrunch hat down on bear's head; glue in place. Glue pom-pom to point of hat.

2. For packages, wrap each foam piece with red or green felt; glue in place. Glue a ribbon length around each package.

3. Use red pen to draw ribbons and stripes on cup. Use green pen to draw dots on cup.

4. Glue bear inside cup.

5. For hanger, twist one end of floral wire around bear's neck; bend remaining end of wire into a loop.

6. Tie remaining red ribbon into a bow around bear's neck, covering wire.

IN ONLY
40
MINUTES!

What better place for Santa than atop the tree! Our muslin fellow adds a cute country touch to the evergreen. His clothes are made using simple patterns, and his face is easy to apply with marking pens.

SANTA TREE TOPPER

You will need: 17"h muslin doll, black fabric paint, paintbrush, wood-tone spray, small muslin drawstring bag, tracing paper, $^3/_8$ yd. of red fabric, natural and bleached wool roving, tan and brown markers, 30" length of jute twine, polyester fiberfill, small sprig of artificial greenery, and a hot glue gun and glue sticks.

1. Paint doll's hands and feet black. Lightly spray drawstring bag with wood-tone spray; allow to dry.

2. Referring to *Making Patterns* (pg. 104), trace Santa coat pattern (pg. 115) onto tracing paper. Cut a 12" x 16" piece of fabric. Matching right sides and short edges, fold fabric in half. Aligning shoulders of pattern with fold of fabric, use pattern to cut out Santa coat.

3. Using a $^1/_4$" seam allowance, stitch underarm and side seams; turn right side out and press. For coat trim, cut one 16" and two 10" lengths of bleached roving; glue 16" length around bottom of coat and one 10" length around each cuff.

4. For pants, cut two 5$^1/_4$" x 10" rectangles from fabric. Place rectangles right sides together. Referring to Fig. 1, stitch side and inner leg seams. Cut up to but not through inside of inner leg seams. Turn right side out and press. For pants trim, cut two 6" lengths of bleached roving; glue one length around bottom of each pants leg.

Fig. 1

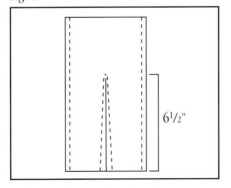

6$^1/_2$"

5. For hood, cut a 5" x 8" rectangle from fabric. Baste along three edges, leaving one 8" edge unstitched. Gather basting

slightly. For hood trim, cut an 8" length of bleached roving; glue along straight edge of hood.

6. Use markers to draw face on doll. For beard, cut a 4" length of natural roving. Stitch across one end of beard to hold in place. Glue beard to doll face.

7. Place clothing on doll, gluing in place where necessary. Tie twine around waist over coat.

8. Stuff drawstring bag with a small amount of fiberfill; place bag on Santa's arm.

9. Glue greenery sprig to one hand.

A personalized ornament is a great way to share holiday cheer with your favorite families! Our hand-painted glass bauble is simple to decorate — a felt-tip pen makes it easy to apply the name and "stitches."

PERSONALIZED ORNAMENT

You will need: tracing paper, 3½" dia. frosted glass ornament, pencil, paintbrush, red and green enamel glass paint, and a black felt-tip pen.

1. Trace star pattern (pg. 123) onto tracing paper; cut out. Carefully cut along lines at center of pattern.

2. Remove hanger from ornament. Place center cuts of pattern over ornament opening and press pattern to ornament. Use pencil to trace around pattern; remove pattern.

3. Center pattern at bottom of ornament and trace around pattern.

4. Paint stars red. Use end of paintbrush to apply dots of green paint at each point of stars. Allow paint to dry.

5. Use pen to draw "stitches" around stars and to write name on ornament.

6. Replace ornament hanger.

This heavenly tree-trimmer smells as good as it looks! Our darling cinnamon angel will dress any evergreen in warm country charm. Easy to create from cinnamon sticks and a foam tube, she'll be a spicy addition to your Christmas decorating.

CINNAMON ANGEL

You will need: serrated knife, 1" dia. foam tube, 2¹/₂" x 4" piece of muslin, ²/₃ yd. of 2¹/₂"w wired ribbon for dress, 4" length of ¹/₄"w flat lace, two 6" long cinnamon sticks, ¹/₂ yd. of 2¹/₂"w mesh wired ribbon for wings, 3" length of floral wire, miniature pinecones, artificial greenery, black pen, red colored pencil, 12" length of ¹/₄"w red satin ribbon, 8" length of clear nylon thread, and a hot glue gun and glue sticks.

1. For doll body, use serrated knife to cut a 4¹/₂" length of foam tube, tapering one end for head.

2. With fabric extending ¹/₂" beyond head end of foam tube, wrap muslin around tube; glue in place. Fold excess fabric over and glue in place.

3. Cut the following pieces from ribbon for dress: one 10" length for skirt, one 4" length for bodice, and two 2¹/₂" lengths for sleeves.

4. Overlapping ends at back, wrap bodice around foam tube; glue in place. For collar, glue flat lace around top of bodice.

5. Holding wire end of one edge of ribbon for skirt, gather ribbon. Adjusting gathers to fit around doll body, twist wires together to secure over bottom of bodice; glue in place.

6. For arms, cut one cinnamon stick in half. Gather ribbon for sleeves. Wrap one sleeve around each arm; glue in place. Glue arms to doll.

7. For legs, insert remaining cinnamon stick into bottom of doll body; glue in place.

8. For wings, bring ends of mesh ribbon to center of ribbon, overlapping ¹/₂". Pinch together and secure with floral wire. Glue wings to back of doll at shoulders.

9. For hair, glue pinecones to doll head. Glue sprig of greenery in hair.

10. Use pen to draw face on doll; use red pencil to color cheeks.

11. Tie satin ribbon into a bow around waist of doll.

12. For hanger, fold nylon thread in half; knot to form a loop. Glue knot to back of ornament.

*L*et a snowy friend decorate
*your tree in frosty style! A papier-
mâché bell is painted and dressed
with "buttons" and a fabric scrap
"scarf" to create the character. He's a
snap to complete in just 10 minutes!*

SNOWMAN BELL ORNAMENT

You will need: white, orange, and black
acrylic paint; 2^1/$_2$"h papier-mâché bell
ornament; three black beads; ^{1}/$_2$" x 9"
torn fabric strip; small nail; two small
twigs; and a hot glue gun and glue sticks.

1. Paint ornament white; allow to dry.

2. Paint an orange dot for nose and black
dots for eyes and mouth.

3. For buttons, glue beads to front
of snowman.

4. For scarf, tie fabric strip around
ornament and glue in place.

5. For arms, use nail to punch a hole in
each side of ornament. Glue end of one
twig into each hole.

*O*ur cool snowman bauble is really on the ball! The decoration is a cinch to make, and it truly captures the spirit of the festive winter months. Use a sponge to stamp the snowman's body on a glass ornament, then hand paint his simple features. Why not make one of these fun fellows for each of your pals!

SNOWMAN ON THE BALL

You will need: tracing paper; compressed craft sponge; 3" dia. red satin-finish glass ornament; small paintbrush; white, orange, and black enamel glass paint; 1/2 yd. of 1/4"w ribbon; and a hot glue gun and glue sticks.

1. Trace small snowman pattern (pg. 122) onto tracing paper; cut out.

2. Referring to *Painting Basics* (pg. 104), use pattern to cut shape from craft sponge. Stamp design on center of ornament; allow to dry.

3. Use orange paint to paint snowman's nose and black paint to paint hat, arms, buttons, feet, and face.

4. Use tip of white paint container to draw snowflakes and dots on ornament around snowman; allow to dry.

5. Tie ribbon into a bow; glue to ornament hanger.

IN ONLY 27 MINUTES!

COOKIE-CUTTER ORNAMENTS

When you need to cook up a batch of unique tree-trimmers in a jiffy, these antique-look ornaments are made to order! The aged patina of the cookie cutters is created using a simple painting technique. For a bit of rustic elegance, finish them with raffia bows.

AGED COOKIE CUTTERS

You will need: black acrylic paint; sponge paintbrush; angel, star, and heart metal cookie cutters; Aleene's Weathered Iron Enhancers™ paint; and natural raffia.

1. Thin black paint with a small amount of water. Use sponge brush to apply a thin coat of black paint to each cookie cutter; allow to dry slightly.

2. Apply one coat of weathering paint over black paint; allow to dry.

3. Cut several 12" lengths of raffia. Tie lengths into a knot around each cookie cutter. Trim ends.

IN ONLY
45
MINUTES!

What a handsome fellow! This friendly, fuzzy reindeer will be a happy addition to the Christmas tree. He's crafted from shaggy felt, and his features are made with felt scraps. Jingle bells wrapped around each antler give our red-nosed friend a merry touch.

REINDEER ORNAMENT

You will need: tracing paper; poster board; fabric marking pencil; batting scraps; brown shaggy felt; scraps of white, red, and black felt; white embroidery floss; small twigs for antlers; wired stem with jingle bells; and a hot glue gun and glue sticks.

1. Trace reindeer upper head, lower head, ear, eye, and nose patterns (pg. 123) onto tracing paper; cut out.

2. Use upper and lower head patterns to cut shapes from poster board and batting. Glue batting to poster board shapes.

3. Cutting $1/2$" outside upper and lower head patterns, cut one of each shape from brown felt. Cut two ears from brown felt.

4. Center and glue felt head shapes over batting side of poster board shapes, wrapping excess to back. Position $1^1/2$" of right side of upper head behind wrong side of lower head; glue in place.

5. Fold ears in half lengthwise. Glue square end of each together; glue to top back of head.

6. Use eye pattern to cut two shapes each from white and black felt. Use nose pattern to cut shape from red felt.

7. Use six strands of white floss to stitch details in black eyes and nose.

8. Glue nose to reindeer lower head; glue white, then black eyes to upper head, overlapping so that small amount of white eyes show.

9. For mouth, cut a $1/4$" x 3" strip and two $1/4$" x $1/2$" strips from black felt. Glue strips in place.

10. For antlers, wrap a length of jingle bell stem around each twig. Glue twigs to back of head.

11. For ornament hanger, cut a 3" length of floral wire; bend to form a loop and glue to top back of head.

12. Use upper and lower head patterns to cut one shape of each from brown felt. Glue upper head, then lower head to back of reindeer.

13. For scarf, cut a $3/4$" x 12" length of red felt; fringe ends. Tie into a loose knot and glue under reindeer's chin.

COLORFUL FELT CANDLE

IN ONLY
15
MINUTES!

With their warm, mood-setting glow, candles are lovely, nostalgic complements to seasonal merriment. Our three-dimensional candle is fashioned from felt and finished with a wooden star and buttons. You can complete one of these heartwarming ornaments in a mere 15 minutes!

FELT CANDLE ORNAMENT

You will need: 4¹/₂" x 12" rectangle of red felt; pinking shears; tracing paper; scraps of yellow, red, and green felt; ¹/₄"w double-fold black bias tape; 1" dia. wooden button; brown felt-tip pen; 3"w wooden star cutout; ³/₈" dia. red button; spring-type clothespin; and a hot glue gun and glue sticks.

1. Trim one short edge of red felt rectangle with pinking shears. Beginning at short unpinked edge, roll rectangle to form candle; glue to secure.

2. Trace large flame, small flame, and holly leaf patterns (pg. 118) onto tracing paper. Use patterns to cut one large flame from yellow felt and one small flame from red felt. Center red flame at bottom of yellow flame; glue in place. Use pattern to cut two holly leaves from green felt.

3. Cut one 6" and two 3" lengths of bias tape. Glue 6" length along edge of yellow flame. Glue one 3" length to each leaf.

4. Glue wooden button to center front of candle over pinked edge.

5. Glue bottom of flame to center top of candle.

6. Use pen to draw dots along edges of wooden star. Glue candle to center of star.

7. Arrange leaves at base of candle; glue in place. Glue red button to point of one leaf.

8. Glue clothespin to bottom of wooden star.

94

*D*ressed *for holiday fun,
our gingerbread girl is a fresh
and folksy way to put a homespun
touch on the tree, a present, or an
evergreen garland. Made by lightly
stuffing two layers of craft paper,
this little miss sports a fused-fabric
dress and a curly wire hanger
decorated with buttons and bows.*

GINGERBREAD GIRL ORNAMENT

You will need: tracing paper, two
$5^1/_2$" x 8" rectangles of brown craft paper,
paper-backed fusible web, scraps of
assorted fabrics, black pen, red colored
pencil, polyester fiberfill, three assorted
buttons, 16" length of floral wire, and
craft glue.

1. Trace outline only of gingerbread girl
pattern (pg. 124) onto tracing paper; cut
out. Use pattern to cut two shapes from
paper rectangles.

2. Referring to *Fusing Basics* (pg. 104),
use body, dress, collar, button, foot, tree,
tree trunk, and cuff patterns (pg. 124) to
make appliqués from assorted fabrics.
Arrange appliqués on one paper shape;
fuse in place.

3. Use pen to draw face, cheeks, and leg
line on gingerbread girl. Use red pencil
to color cheeks.

4. Glue edges of paper shapes together,
leaving opening for stuffing. Stuff
ornament lightly with fiberfill; glue
opening closed.

5. Thread buttons onto floral wire, loosely
curling sections of wire between buttons
by wrapping around pencil. Insert ends of
wire through shoulders of ornament and
bend ends to secure.

6. Tear four $^1/_2$" x 2" strips of fabric. Knot
three lengths around wire. For hair bow,
knot center of remaining fabric strip; glue
in place.

The prettiest babies on the block will look picture-perfect when they're featured on these bunting ornaments. A sweet way to share baby's photo with relatives, the ribbon-trimmed charmers are precious accents on the tree or on gifts.

BABY'S FIRST CHRISTMAS ORNAMENT

For each ornament, you will need: two 4¹/₂" x 6" rectangles of paper-backed fusible web and one each of felt, fabric, and poster board; tracing paper; baby picture; ¹/₄"w flat lace trim; black fine-point pen; ¹/₄"w satin ribbon; and glue.

1. Referring to *Fusing Basics* (pg. 104), fuse poster board rectangle between fabric and felt rectangles.

2. Trace baby ornament pattern (pg. 123) onto tracing paper; cut out. Use pattern to cut ornament from fused rectangle.

3. Cut face from baby picture and glue to ornament; allow to dry. Cut a length of lace trim to fit around face. Glue in place and allow to dry.

4. Use pen to draw "stitches" and write message on ornament.

5. To make each small bow, tie a knot in satin ribbon; trim ribbon ¹/₂" from each side of knot. Glue three bows to center front of ornament; allow to dry.

6. To make larger bow, tie a 6" length of ribbon into a bow; trim ends. Glue bow to bottom of ornament; allow to dry.

7. For hanger, cut an 8" length of ribbon. Form a loop and glue ends to back of ornament; allow to dry.

*O*ur wooden spoon angel spreads holiday cheer and whimsical charm from her lofty perch atop the tree. Dressed up with assorted buttons and flyaway twig hair, the quick-to-complete angel can also shine as a package decoration.

BUTTON ANGEL

You will need: antique white acrylic paint; paintbrush; wooden spoon; two jumbo craft sticks; two 4¹/₄" long wooden heart cutouts; 10" squares of foam core board, ecru fabric, and paper-backed fusible web; tracing paper; craft knife; black felt-tip marker; pink colored pencil; small twigs; 1¹/₂" dia. white shank button; 9" length of 1¹/₂"w flat ecru lace; assorted buttons; 6" length of floral wire; and a hot glue gun and glue sticks.

1. Apply one coat of white paint to one side of wooden spoon, craft sticks, and heart cutouts; allow to dry.

2. Referring to *Fusing Basics* (pg. 104), use web to fuse wrong side of fabric to foam core board.

3. Trace large angel body pattern (pg. 127) onto tracing paper; cut out. Draw around pattern on fused foam core board; use craft knife to cut out shape.

4. Use marker to draw eyes and mouth on spoon for doll face and to draw shoes on craft sticks. Use pink pencil to color cheeks.

5. For hair, glue several twigs to top of spoon. For halo, glue white shank button to top back of spoon.

6. Glue lace 1" from bottom of body, wrapping ends to back. Glue buttons to body; glue one small button over each shoe.

7. Glue spoon handle, tips of hearts (wings), and 2¹/₂" of each craft stick (legs) to back of body.

8. For hanger, fold floral wire in half to form a loop; twist ends together. Glue to back of spoon near tips of wings.

JINGLE BELL BAUBLE

*S*hort on gift-making time before the club party? This fast and easy ornament will make you the "bell of the bough!" It only takes a few minutes to top a large jingle bell with gathered ribbon, faux greenery, and a silk poinsettia. Add a satin ribbon hanger, and you'll be ready to jingle all the way.

JINGLE BELL ORNAMENT

You will need: 18" length of 2$\frac{1}{2}$"w wired ribbon, 4" dia. jingle bell, small poinsettia pick, artificial greenery, 10" length of $\frac{1}{4}$"w green satin ribbon, and a hot glue gun and glue sticks.

1. Holding one end of wire, gather ribbon tightly along one edge. Twist ends of wire together to secure. Glue gathered edge of ribbon around top of jingle bell.

2. Cut several sprigs from poinsettia pick and greenery; glue around hanger over ribbon.

3. Thread green satin ribbon through hanger on bell. Tie a knot 1" from ends of ribbon to form hanging loop.

IN ONLY
8
MINUTES!

IN ONLY
30
MINUTES!

*C*reativity is the most important tool needed for these special tokens — they're easy enough that even kids can join in the fun! The festive designs are "painted" onto glass balls using permanent markers, then blended using a cotton swab. The golden details are added with a paint pen.

HAND-PAINTED GLASS ORNAMENTS

You will need: pearl white glass ornaments; red and green wide-tip permanent markers; red, blue, and green fine-tip permanent markers; cotton swabs; and a gold paint pen.

1. Remove hangers from ornaments.

2. Use wide-tip markers to draw designs on ornaments as desired. Use cotton swab to blend ink before it dries; draw over design with fine-tip markers.

3. Use gold paint pen to add details to each ornament; allow to dry.

4. Replace hangers.

IN ONLY
30
MINUTES!

What a wondrous delight! These fancy ornaments glitter and gleam with gold, red, and green jewels. And surprisingly enough, you can make one in just a half-hour! Pearled gold dimensional paint adds sparkle to our filigree designs, which are cut from clear plastic.

FILIGREE ORNAMENTS

For each ornament, you will need: clear shrink-art plastic; removable tape; assorted gold, red, and green acrylic jewels; tacky glue; pearlized gold dimensional paint; hole punch; and an 8" length of ¼"w gold ribbon.

1. Place plastic directly over desired ornament pattern (pg. 124 or 125); tape in place.

2. Referring to pattern for placement, glue jewels to plastic.

3. Apply paint onto plastic over lines of pattern and around jewels; allow to dry.

4. Cut out ornament along outer edge of design.

5. Punch a hole at top of ornament.

6. For hanger, thread ribbon through hole, matching ends; tie in a knot.

BUTTONED-UP PHOTO ORNAMENT

IN ONLY
3 1
MINUTES!

Showcase a precious portrait in this unique frame ornament embellished with an assortment of gold buttons. Foam core board wrapped in gold ribbon provides the base for this elegant project, and a darling picture gives it extra charm.

GOLD BUTTON FRAME ORNAMENT
You will need: drawing compass, 4" square of foam core board, craft knife, 1 yd. of $^{7}/_{8}$"w gold satin ribbon, 3" square of poster board, desired photo, assorted gold buttons, $^{3}/_{8}$ yd. of $1^{3}/_{8}$"w gold mesh ribbon, $^{1}/_{2}$ yd. of $^{1}/_{4}$"w gold mesh ribbon, and a hot glue gun and glue sticks.

1. For frame, use compass to draw a $3^{1}/_{4}$" dia. circle on foam core board. Draw a $1^{3}/_{4}$" circle in center of $3^{1}/_{4}$" circle. Use craft knife to cut out frame.

2. Wrap frame with gold satin ribbon to cover completely; glue ends in place.

3. Glue buttons to frame, overlapping to cover completely.

4. Draw a 3" dia. circle on poster board; cut out. Use poster board circle as a pattern to cut 3" circle from desired area of photo. Glue poster board circle to back of photo circle. Center photo on back of frame and glue in place.

5. Tie $1^{3}/_{8}$"w gold mesh ribbon into a bow; trim ends.

6. For hanger, fold $^{1}/_{4}$"w mesh ribbon in half. Tie a knot $1^{3}/_{4}$" from fold. Glue bow to knot. Glue streamers to back of frame ornament.

101

AROUND THE BLOCK WITH SANTA

*H*eartwarming images of Kris Kringle, snipped from gift wrap, give our antique-look tree-trimmer a nostalgic look. Gold beads, ribbon, and a tassel add the final touches to the quick 14-minute project.

WOODEN SANTA BLOCK ORNAMENT
You will need: three 1¹/₂" square wooden blocks, Santa-pattern gift wrap, decoupage glue, craft knife, wood-tone spray, 12" length of ³/₈"w gold ribbon, gold spray paint, two 1" dia. wooden beads, gold tassel, and a hot glue gun and glue sticks.

1. Place blocks together end to end. Cut four different Santa figures from gift wrap. Use decoupage glue to glue one Santa to each side of blocks, overlapping at corners if necessary; allow glue to dry. To separate blocks, use craft knife to cut paper between blocks.

2. Lightly spray blocks with wood-tone spray; allow to dry.

3. Cut two 1" pieces of ribbon. Center and hot glue one end of one piece to top of center block and one end of remaining piece to bottom of center block. Glue remaining end of top strip to bottom of top block; glue remaining end of bottom strip to top of bottom block.

4. Spray paint beads gold; allow to dry.

5. Cut a 2" strip of ribbon. Thread tassel loop through one bead; thread ribbon through loop of tassel. Glue ends of ribbon to bottom of bottom block.

6. Cut two 8" lengths of ribbon; fold one length in half. Glue ends to top of top block. Thread bead onto folded ribbon; tie a knot in ribbon at top of bead.

7. Tie remaining 8" length of ribbon into a bow; glue to top of ornament near hanger.

102

SOFT-TOUCH SNOWMAN

IN ONLY 15 MINUTES!

*E*ven before the first flurries fall, you can have fun building a jaunty snowman ornament. A white terry washcloth wrapped around a foam ball creates the look of snow. Felt features and a toy top hat give this fellow his jolly personality.

TERRY SNOWMAN

You will need: 3" dia. foam ball, white terry washcloth, rubber band, tracing paper, scraps of orange and black felt, 1/8"w red satin ribbon for hanger and bow, small top hat to fit foam ball, 1/4"w red grosgrain ribbon for hatband, three small artificial holly berries, and a hot glue gun and glue sticks.

1. For head, center foam ball on washcloth. Wrap washcloth tightly around ball and secure with rubber band. Cut off excess washcloth.

2. Trace nose pattern (pg. 124) onto tracing paper; cut one shape from orange felt. Roll nose into a cone shape and glue to secure.

3. Cut eight small pieces of black felt for eyes and mouth. Glue nose, mouth pieces, and eyes to head.

4. For hanger, cut a 9" length of satin ribbon; glue ends to top of hat, forming a loop. Tie a 6" length of satin ribbon into a small bow; glue over ends of hanger.

5. Glue hatband and holly berries to hat. Glue hat to snowman head, covering rubber band and raw edges of washcloth.

General Instructions

Adhesives

When using any adhesive, carefully follow the manufacturer's instructions.

White craft glue: Recommended for paper. Dry flat.

Tacky craft glue: Recommended for paper, fabric, floral, or wood. Dry flat or secure items with clothespins or straight pins until glue is dry.

Fabric glue: Recommended for fabric or paper. Dry flat or secure items with clothespins or straight pins until glue is dry.

Decoupage glue: Recommended for decoupaging fabric or paper to a surface such as wood or glass. Use purchased decoupage glue or mix one part craft glue with one part water.

Hot or low-temperature glue gun: Recommended for floral, paper, fabric, or wood. Hold in place until set. A low-temperature glue gun is safer than a hot glue gun, but the bond made with the glue is not as strong.

Making Patterns

(**Note:** To make a more durable pattern, draw around tracing paper pattern on translucent vinyl template material; cut out.)

Half-patterns: Fold tracing paper in half. Place fold along dashed line and trace pattern half; turn folded paper over and draw over traced lines on remaining side. Unfold pattern; cut out.

Two-part patterns: Trace one part of pattern onto tracing paper. Match dotted line and arrows of traced part with dotted line and arrows of second part in book and trace second part; cut out.

Fusing Basics

(**Note:** To protect your ironing board, cover with muslin. Web material that sticks to iron may be removed with hot iron cleaner, available at fabric and craft stores.)

Using fusible web: Place web side of paper-backed fusible web on wrong side of fabric. Follow manufacturer's instructions to fuse web to fabric. Remove paper backing. Position fused fabric web side down on project and press with heated iron for ten seconds. Repeat, lifting and repositioning iron until all fabric is fused.

Making fusible fabric appliqués: (**Note:** To prevent darker fabrics from showing though, white or light-colored fabrics may need to be lined with fusible interfacing before being fused.)

Trace appliqué pattern onto paper side of web. When making more than one appliqué, leave at least 1" between shapes. Cutting ½" outside drawn shape, cut out web shape. Fuse to wrong side of fabric. Cut out shape along drawn lines. Remove paper backing. If pattern is a half-pattern or to make a reversed appliqué, make a tracing paper pattern (turn traced pattern over for reversed appliqué) and follow instructions using traced pattern.

Foil method: When applying fusible web to items that are narrow or openwork items (lace, doilies, etc.), place a piece of foil shiny side up under items to prevent web from sticking to ironing board. Place item wrong side up on foil. Place web paper side up over item; press. Peel item from foil; trim excess web. Remove paper backing and fuse to project.

Painting Basics

Painting with a sponge piece: Pour a small amount of paint onto a paper plate. Dip dampened sponge piece into paint and remove excess on a paper towel. Use a light stamping motion to apply paint. Reapply paint to sponge as necessary. Allow painted item to dry. If desired, repeat with a second coat or another color.

Painting with a sponge shape: Use a pen to draw around pattern on a dry compressed craft sponge; cut out shape. Dampen sponge shape to expand. Pour a small amount of paint onto a paper plate. Dip one side of sponge shape into paint and remove excess on a paper towel. Lightly press sponge shape on project, then carefully lift. Reapplying paint to sponge shape as necessary, repeat to paint additional shapes on project.

Stenciling: For stencil, cut a piece of template material at least 1" larger on all sides than pattern. Place template material directly over pattern in book. Use a pen to trace pattern onto template material. Place template material on cutting mat and use craft knife to cut out stencil segments, making sure edges are smooth.

Pour a small amount of paint onto a paper plate. Hold or tape (using removable tape) stencil in place on project. Dip a stencil brush or sponge piece in paint and remove excess on a paper towel. Brush or sponge should be almost dry to produce good results. Beginning at edge of cut-out area, apply paint in a stamping motion over stencil. Carefully remove stencil from project. To stencil a design in reverse, clean stencil and turn stencil over.

Sealing: If an item will be handled frequently or used outdoors, we recommend sealing the item with clear acrylic sealer. Sealers are available in spray or brush-on form in several finishes. Follow manufacturer's instructions to apply sealer.

Painting with dimensional paint: Turn bottle upside down to fill tip before each use. While painting, clean tip often with a paper towel. If tip becomes clogged, insert a straight pin into opening to unclog.

To paint, touch tip to project. Squeezing and moving bottle steadily, apply paint to project, being careful not to flatten paint line. If securing an appliqué, center line of paint to cover raw edge of appliqué. If painting detail lines, center line of paint over transferred line on project or freehand details as desired.

To correct a mistake, use a paring knife to gently scrape excess paint from project before it dries. Carefully remove stain with non-acetone nail polish remover on a cotton swab. A mistake may also be camouflaged by incorporating it into the design.

EMBROIDERY STITCHES

Straight Stitch: Referring to Fig. 1, bring needle up at 1 and go down at 2.

Fig. 1

Running Stitch: Referring to Fig. 2, make a series of straight stitches with stitch length equal to the space between stitches.

Fig. 2

Blanket Stitch: Referring to Figs. 3 and 4, bring needle up at 1. Keeping thread below point of needle, go down at 2 and come up at 3. Continue working as shown.

Fig. 3   Fig. 4

French Knot: Referring to Fig. 5, bring needle up at 1. Wrap floss once around needle and insert needle at 2, holding end of floss with non-stitching fingers. Tighten knot, then pull needle through fabric, holding floss until it must be released. For a larger knot, use more strands; wrap only once.

Fig.5

MULTI-LOOP BOWS

Making a multi-loop bow: For first streamer, measure desired length of streamer from one end of ribbon and twist ribbon between fingers.

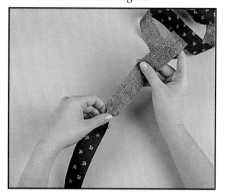

For first loop, keep right side of ribbon facing out and fold ribbon to front to form desired-size loop; gather between fingers.

Fold ribbon to back to form another loop; gather between fingers. Continue to form loops, varying size as desired, until bow is desired size.

For remaining streamer, trim ribbon to desired length.

Follow project instructions to secure bow. If project instructions don't indicate a method for securing bow, wrap a length of wire around center of bow with ends at back. Hold wire ends with one hand and twist bow with the other hand to tighten wire. If desired, wrap a short length of ribbon around bow center and glue ends together at back, covering wire. Use wire ends to secure bow to project or trim ends close to bow and glue bow to project.

Arrange loops and trim ribbon ends as desired.

CUTTING A FABRIC CIRCLE

Matching right sides, fold fabric square in half from top to bottom and in half again from left to right.

Refer to project instructions for diameter of fabric circle; determine radius of circle by dividing diameter in half. Tie one end of string to fabric marking pencil. Insert thumbtack through string the determined radius from pencil. Insert thumbtack through fabric as shown in Fig. 1 and mark cutting line. Cut along drawn line through all fabric layers. Unfold circle.

Fig. 1

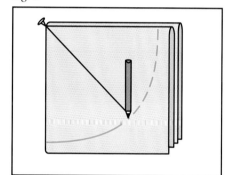

PATTERNS

CANVAS VESTS

VEST STAR

VEST TREE

VEST HEART

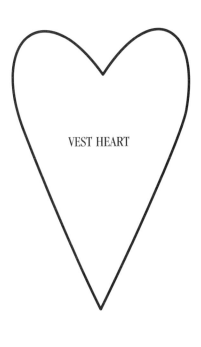

CHRISTMAS CUTIE'S DRESS

YULETIDE SLIPPERS

SLIPPER ORNAMENT

ORNAMENT TOP

BALL ORNAMENT

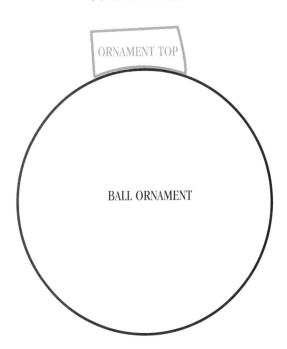

PATTERNS (continued)

FESTIVE COASTERS

SANTA'S
HELPER SMOCK

HOLLY
WITH BERRIES

COLLAR

LARGE SNOWFLAKE

SNOWFLAKE
PILLOWCASES

SMALL SNOWFLAKE

STAR-BRIGHT SCRAPBOOK

STAR

TREE

TREE

TREE TRUNK

PATTERNS (continued)

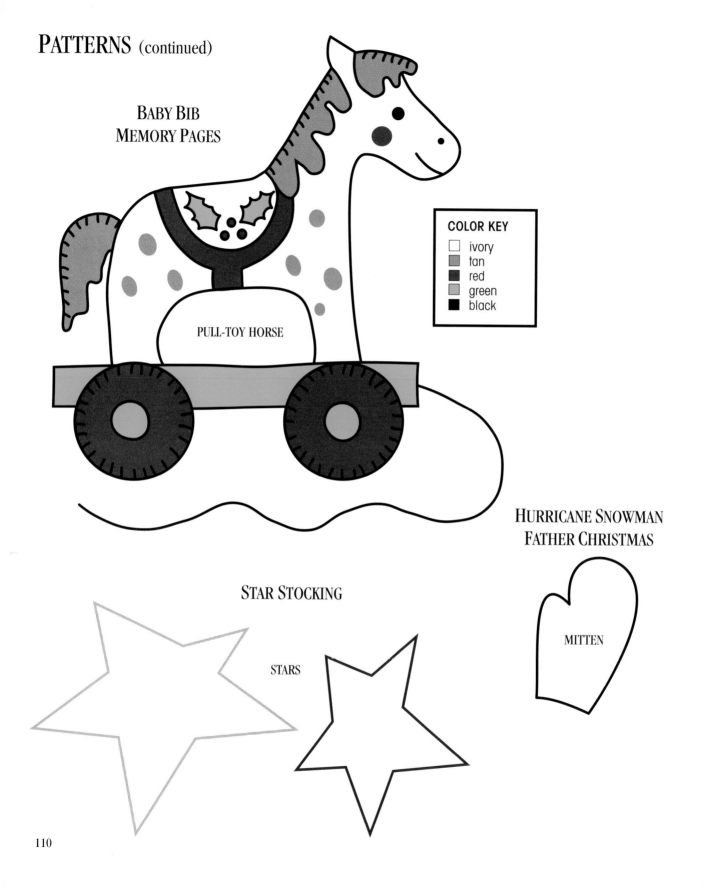

BABY BIB
MEMORY PAGES

PULL-TOY HORSE

COLOR KEY
☐ ivory
☐ tan
☐ red
☐ green
☐ black

HURRICANE SNOWMAN
FATHER CHRISTMAS

STAR STOCKING

STARS

MITTEN

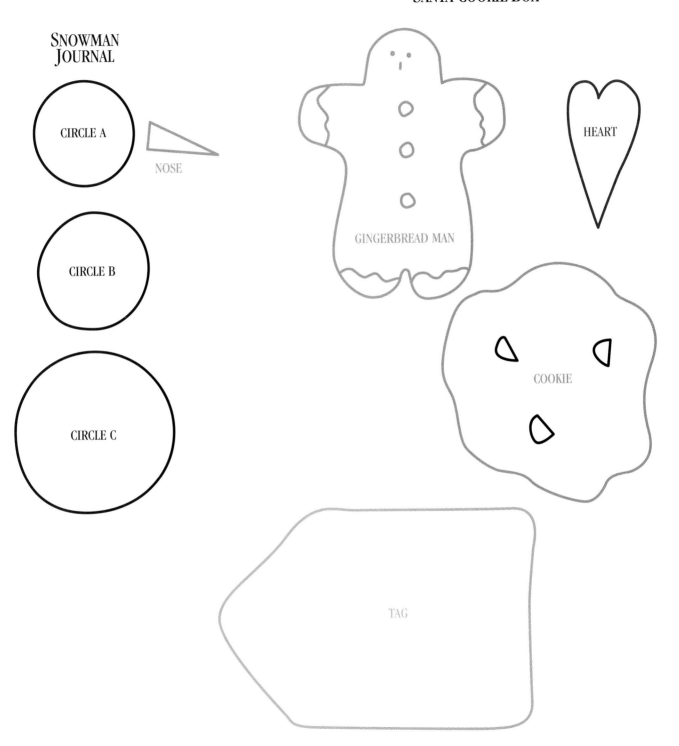

GINGERBREAD MAN MINI TOTE
SANTA COOKIE BOX

SNOWMAN
JOURNAL

CIRCLE A

NOSE

CIRCLE B

CIRCLE C

GINGERBREAD MAN

HEART

COOKIE

TAG

PATTERNS (continued)

SNOWMEN SWEATSHIRT
CHEERY GIFT BAGS

CHRISTMAS BERRY ANGEL

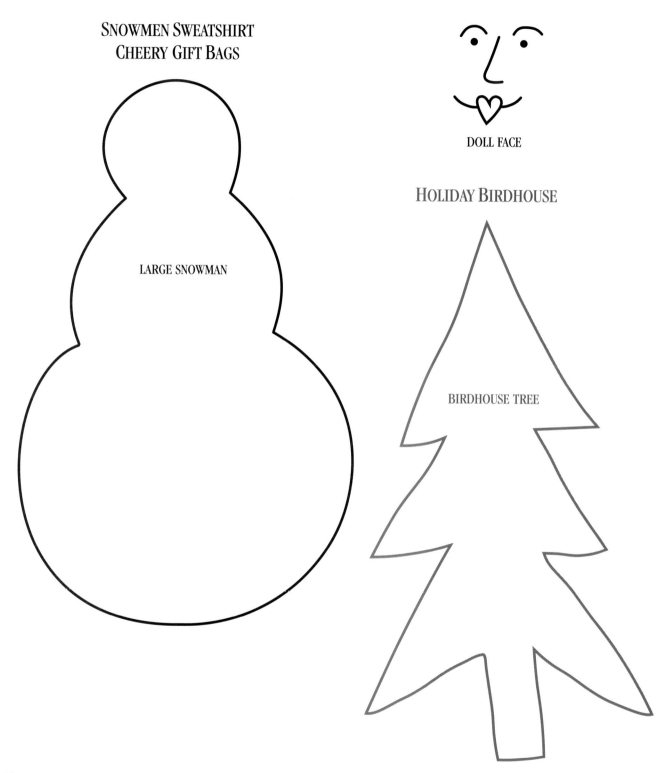

DOLL FACE

LARGE SNOWMAN

HOLIDAY BIRDHOUSE

BIRDHOUSE TREE

FROSTY SWEATSHIRT
SNOWMAN WREATH

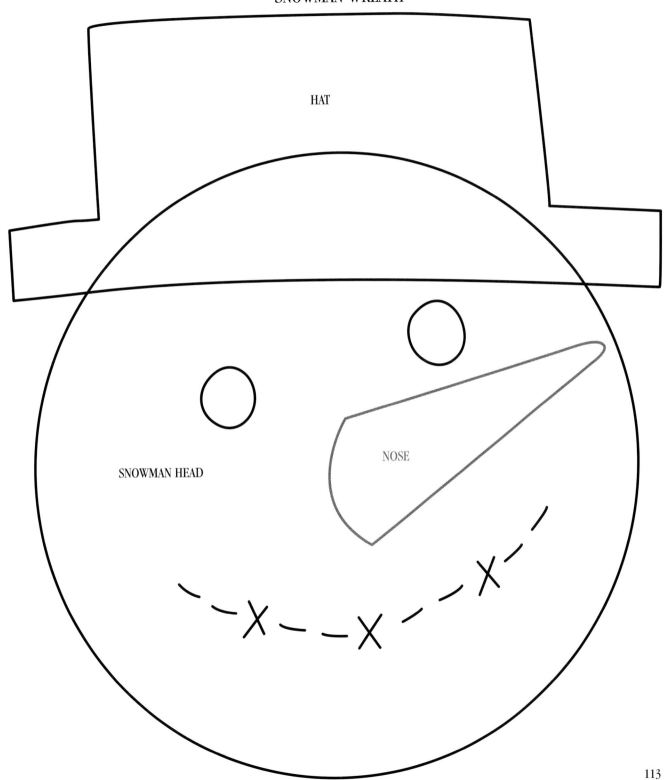

HAT

SNOWMAN HEAD

NOSE

PATTERNS (continued)

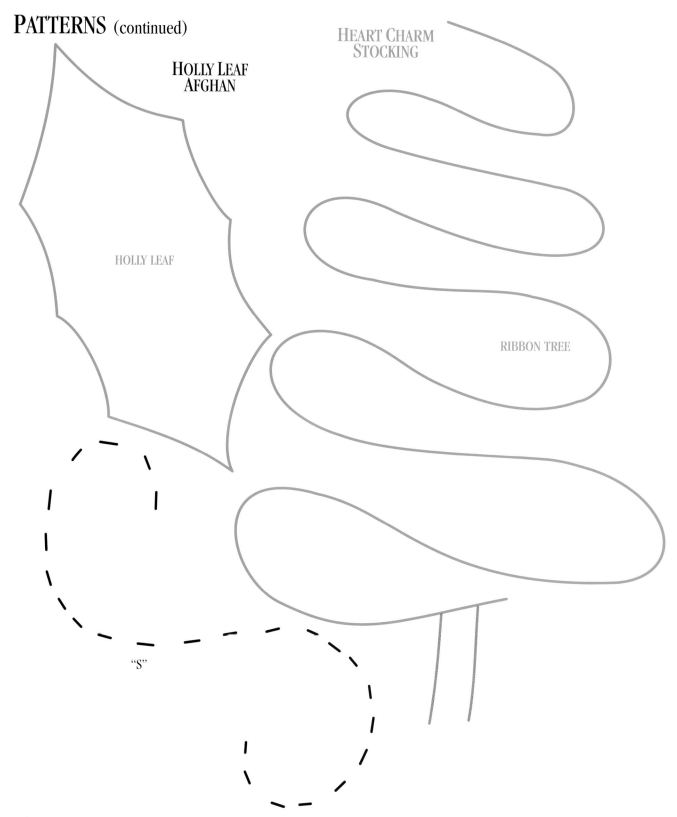

HOLLY LEAF
AFGHAN

HEART CHARM
STOCKING

HOLLY LEAF

RIBBON TREE

"S"

SNOWMAN GARLAND

SNOWMAN HEAD

NOSE

HEART

SANTA TREE TOPPER

BOW TIE

SANTA COAT

PATTERNS (continued)

NOEL BANNER
FESTIVE LAMPSHADE

BANNER

LEAF

NOEL LETTERS

HANDPRINT WALL HANGING

BANNER

HEART

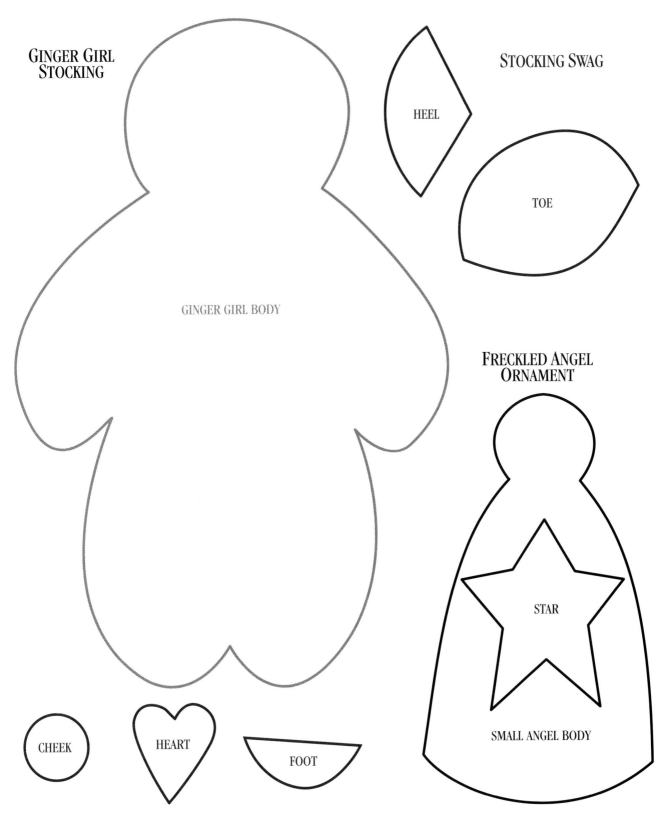

GINGER GIRL
STOCKING

STOCKING SWAG

HEEL

TOE

GINGER GIRL BODY

FRECKLED ANGEL
ORNAMENT

STAR

SMALL ANGEL BODY

CHEEK

HEART

FOOT

PATTERNS (continued)

CHRISTMAS TREE KITCHEN TOWEL

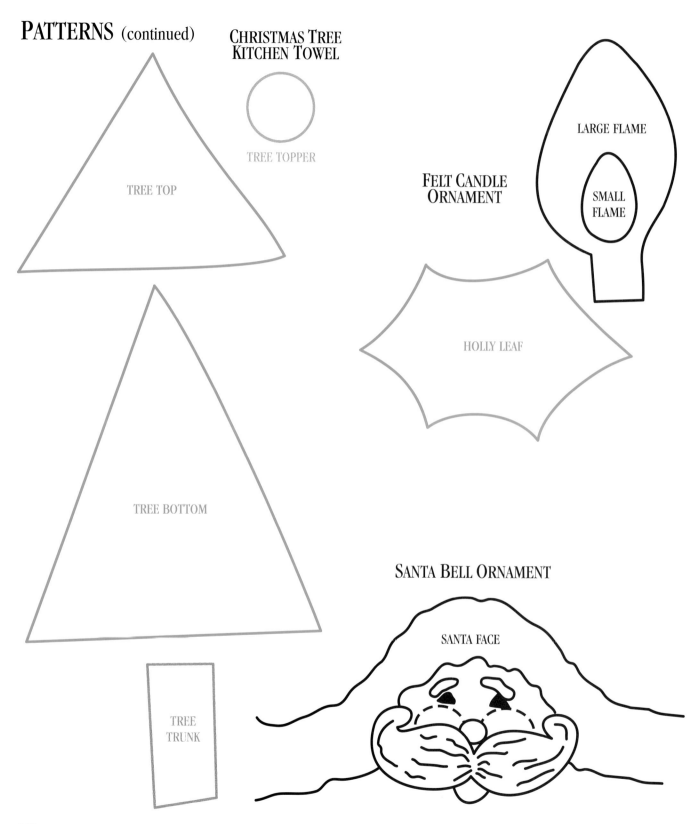

TREE TOP

TREE TOPPER

TREE BOTTOM

TREE TRUNK

FELT CANDLE ORNAMENT

LARGE FLAME

SMALL FLAME

HOLLY LEAF

SANTA BELL ORNAMENT

SANTA FACE

YULETIDE BANNER

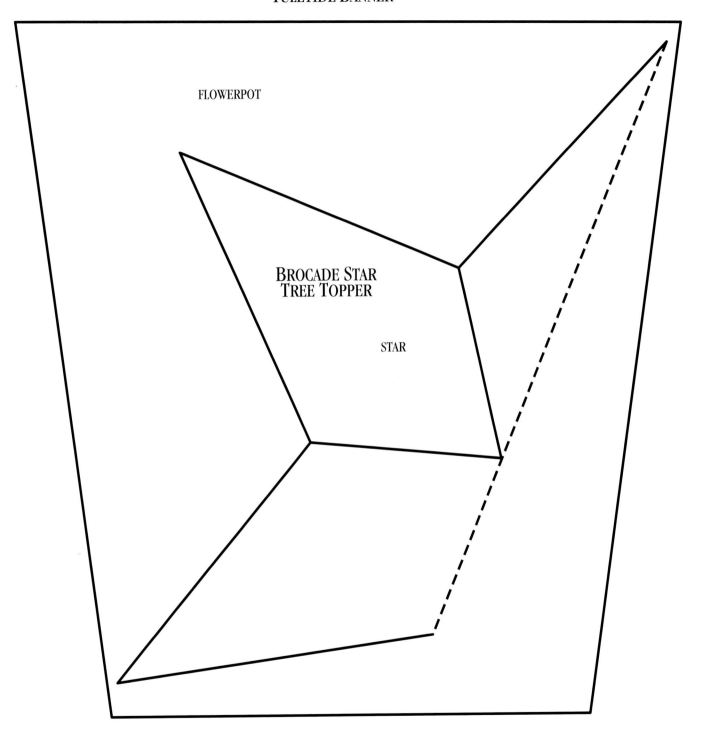

FLOWERPOT

BROCADE STAR
TREE TOPPER

STAR

PATTERNS (continued)

MAGIC SANTA ORNAMENT

BEARD

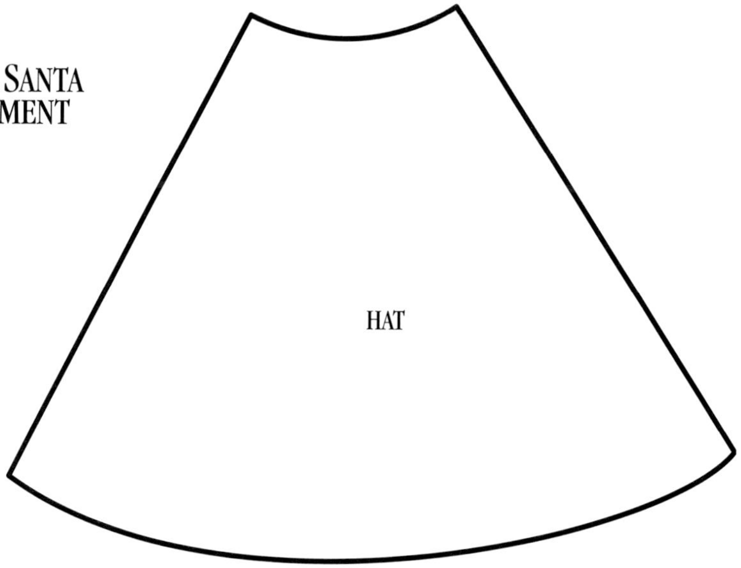

HAT

SNOW LADY TREE

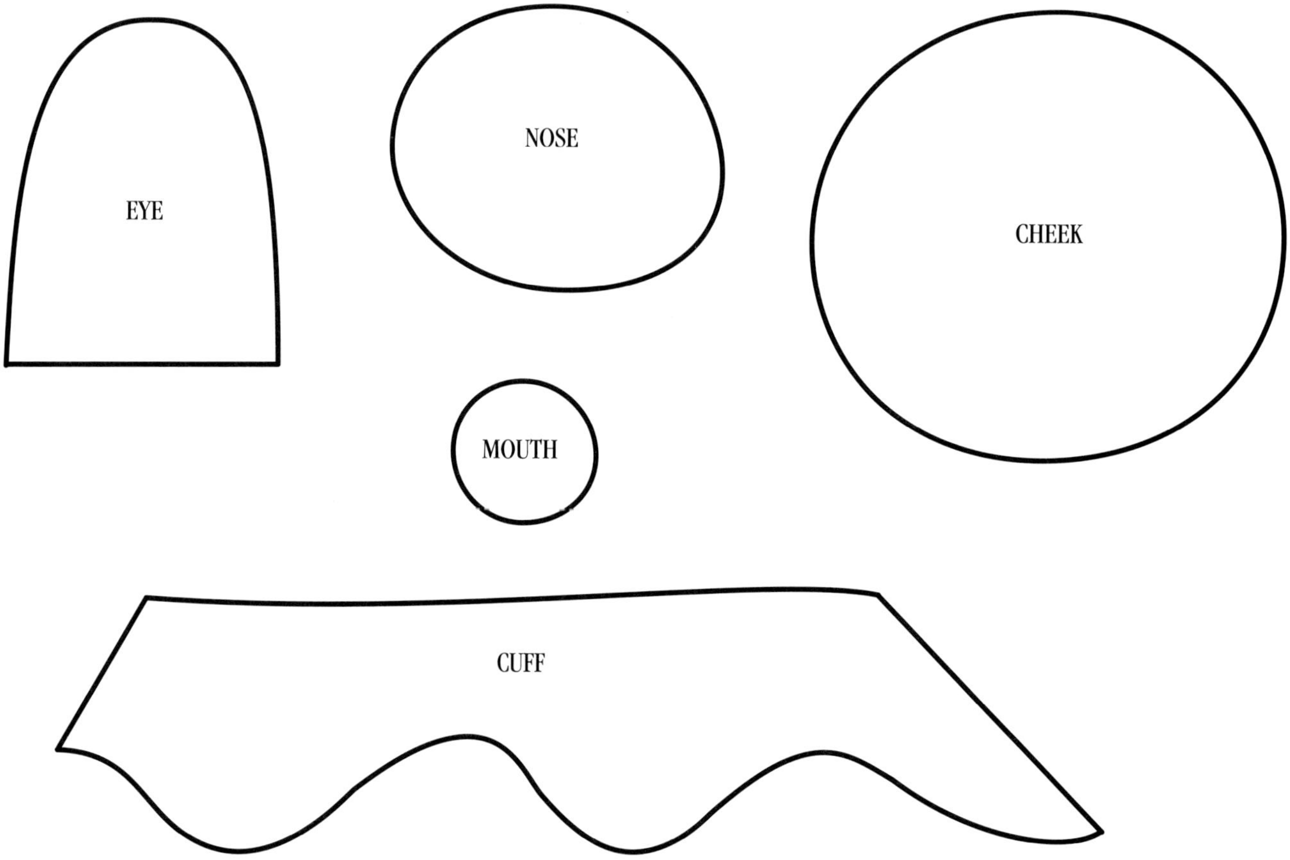

EYE

NOSE

CHEEK

MOUTH

CUFF

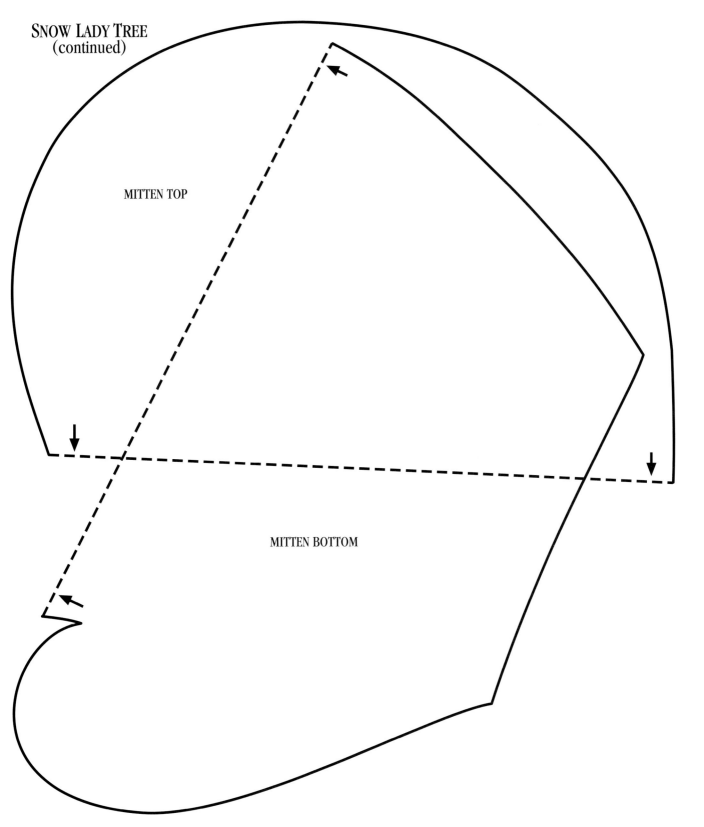

MITTEN TOP

MITTEN BOTTOM

PATTERNS (continued)

ELEGANT TREE SKIRT
MEMORY PAGES

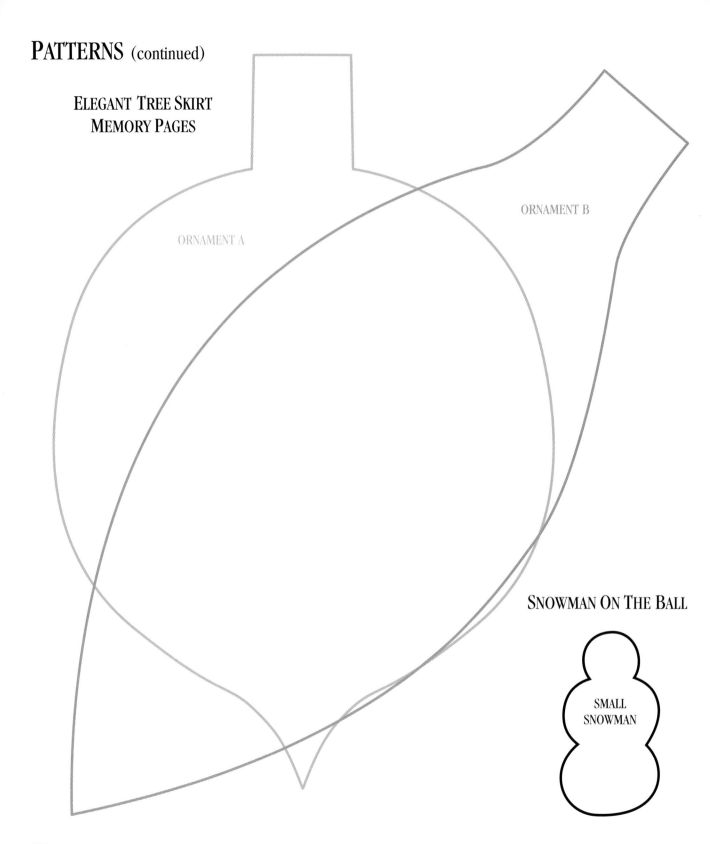

ORNAMENT A

ORNAMENT B

SNOWMAN ON THE BALL

SMALL
SNOWMAN

REINDEER ORNAMENT

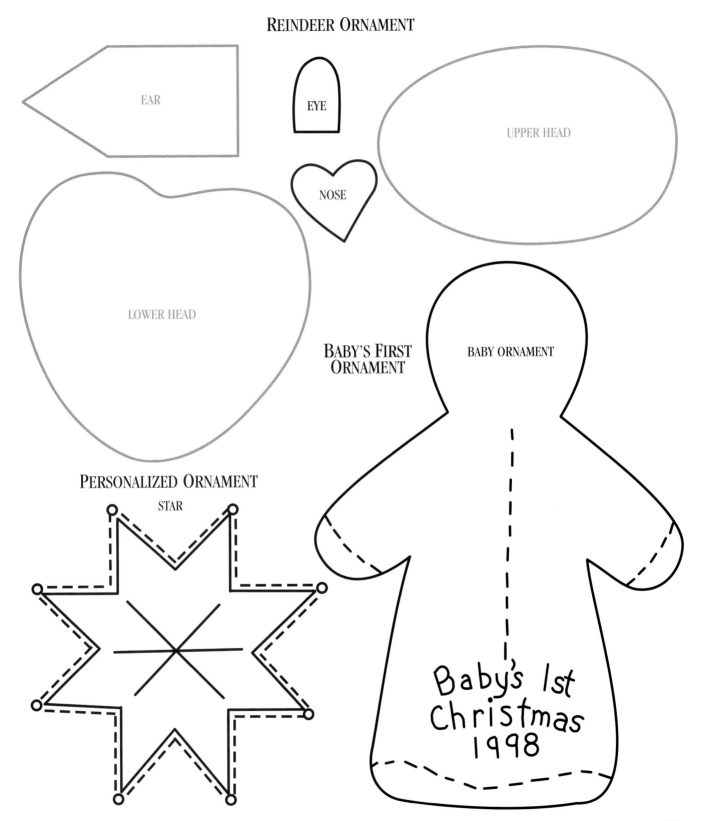

EAR

EYE

UPPER HEAD

NOSE

LOWER HEAD

BABY'S FIRST
ORNAMENT

BABY ORNAMENT

PERSONALIZED ORNAMENT

STAR

Baby's 1st
Christmas
1998

PATTERNS (continued)

FILIGREE ORNAMENTS

FILIGREE ORNAMENT A

GINGERBREAD GIRL ORNAMENT

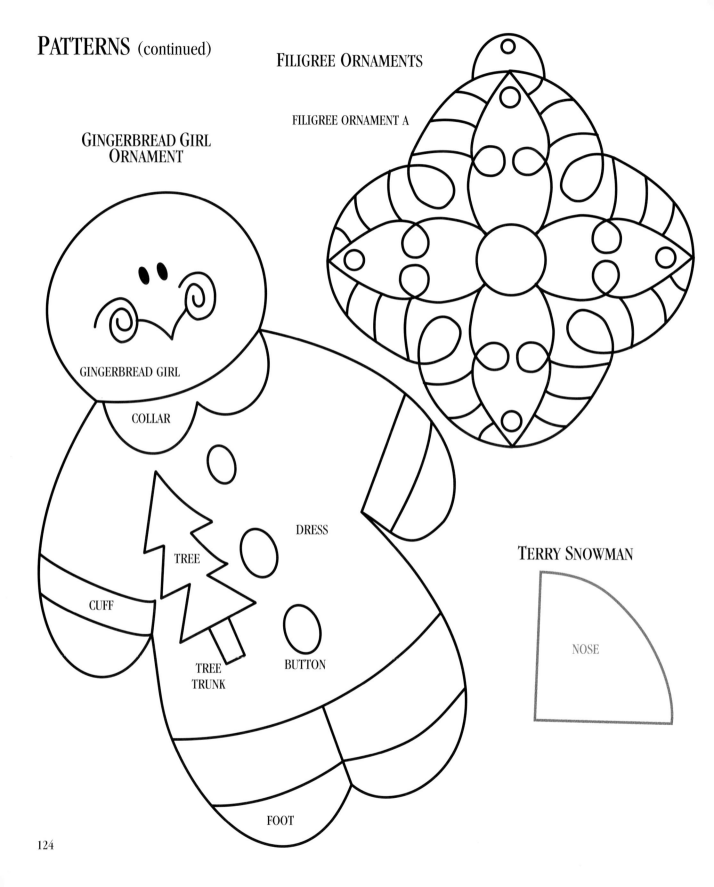

GINGERBREAD GIRL

COLLAR

DRESS

TREE

CUFF

TREE TRUNK

BUTTON

TERRY SNOWMAN

NOSE

FOOT

FILIGREE ORNAMENTS
(continued)

FILIGREE ORNAMENT B

FILIGREE ORNAMENT C

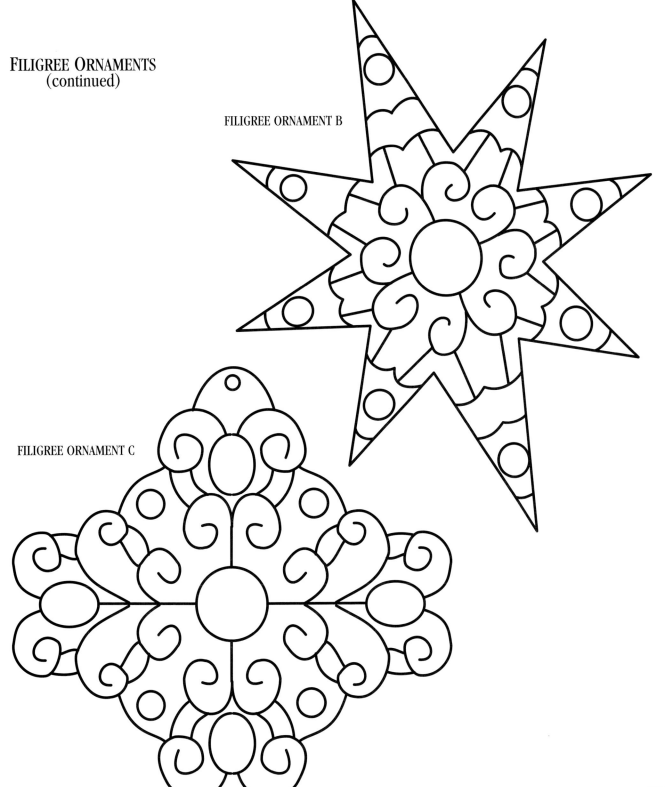

PATTERNS (continued)

BUTTON JEWELRY

SNOWMAN NECKLACE

TREE PIN

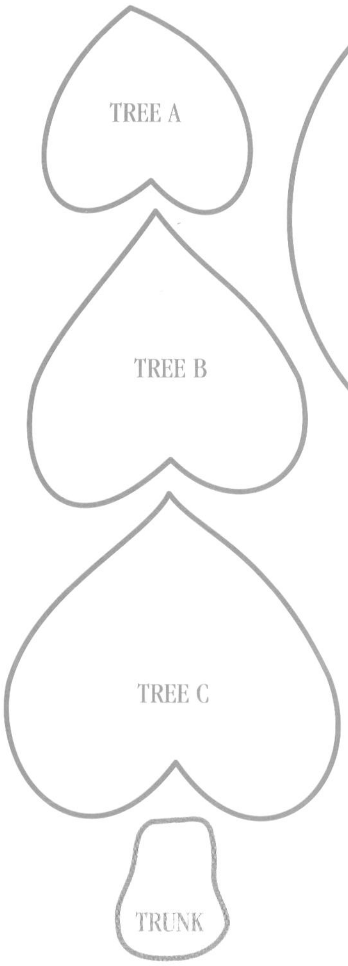

TREE A

TREE B

TREE C

TRUNK

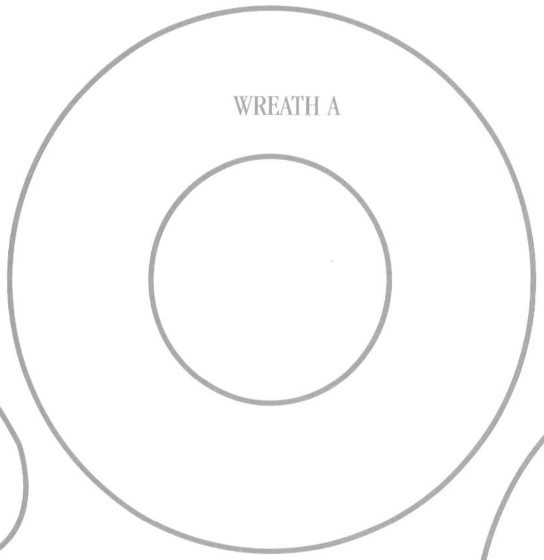

WREATH A

WREATH PIN

WREATH B

POM-POM

HAT

HAT TRIM

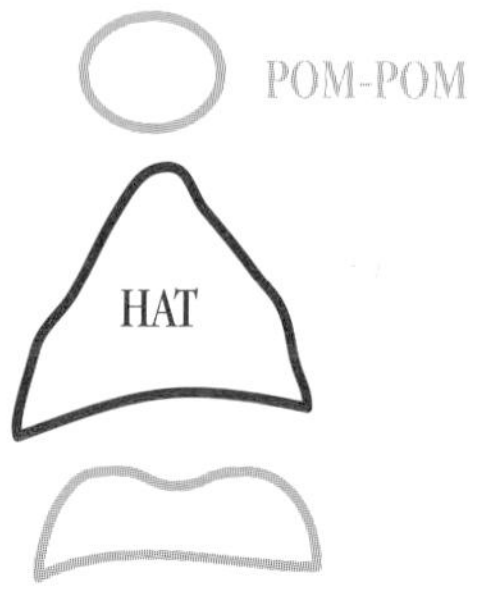

TEACUP BEAR

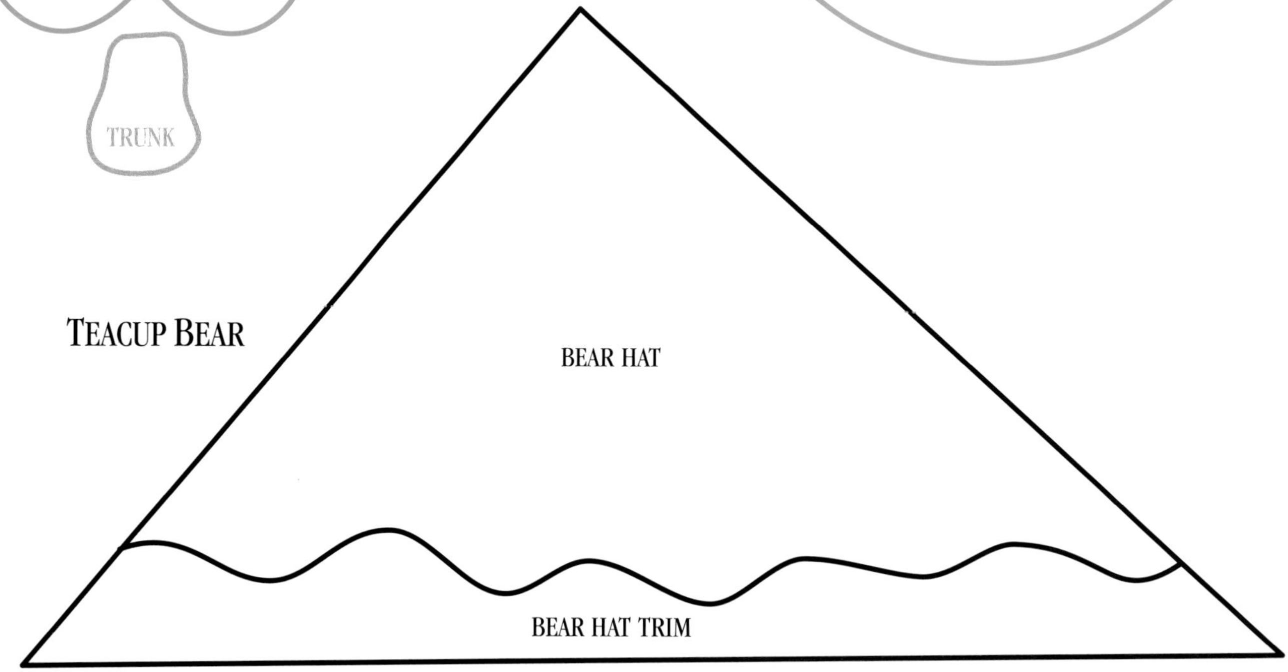

BEAR HAT

BEAR HAT TRIM

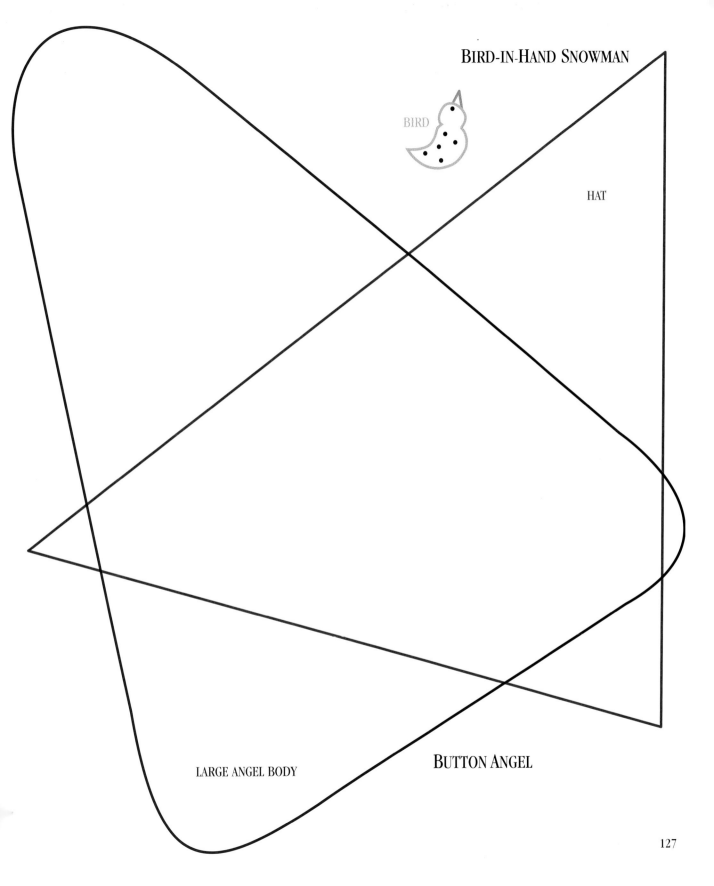

BIRD-IN-HAND SNOWMAN

BIRD

HAT

LARGE ANGEL BODY

BUTTON ANGEL

127

CREDITS

We want to extend a warm *thank you* to the generous people who allowed us to photograph our projects in their homes: James and Joan Adams, Dr. Dan and Sandra Cook, Dennis and Tricia Hendrix, Ellison and Joe Madden, Charles and Peg Mills, Thomas and Julie Mullins, Duncan and Nancy Porter, Dr. Reed and Becky Thompson, and Paul and Ann Weaver.

To Magna IV Color Imaging of Little Rock, Arkansas, we say thank you for the superb color reproduction and excellent pre-press preparation.

We especially want to recognize photographers David Hale, Mark Mathews, Larry Pennington, Karen Shirey, and Ken West of Peerless Photography, and Jerry R. Davis of Jerry Davis Photography, all of Little Rock, Arkansas, for their time, patience, and excellent work.

Leisure Arts would like to thank Viking Husqvarna Sewing Machine Company of Cleveland, Ohio, for providing the sewing machines used to make some of the projects in this book.